| VULGARITER BEGHINAE |

Hans Geybels

VULGARITER
BEGHINAE

Eight Centuries of Beguine History
in the Low Countries

BREPOLS

I CONTENTS I

| INTRODUCTION |

TODAY, THE FEW REMAINING BEGUINES IN BELGIUM ARE all elderly women. Their death will also mean the end of the beguine movement, a spiritual history lasting eight centuries that has mainly been focused in the late-medieval and early-modern Low Countries. The movement emerged during the twelfth century and spread through western Europe. Almost all members were women. Although the first women whose names were known, were all of noble descent or high-born, they returned to the ideals of Jesus and his early disciples, as followers of the movement committing themselves to a life of chastity and solitude, the *vita apostolica*. The movement emerged in the former principality of Liège. It flourished and spread to the duchy of Brabant and the former county of Flanders, in what is today Belgium. In the first quarter of the fourteenth century, the movement had two thousand members in West Germanic-speaking lands.[1]

1. G.-M. OURY, *Dictionnaire des ordres religieux* (Chambray, 1988), p. 41. General: K. ELM, R. SPRANDEL & R. MANSELLI, 'Beg(h)inen', *Lexikon des Mittelalters* (Munich and Zürich, 1977), vol. 1, col. 1799-1803.

In Belgium, many folk tales and popular expressions involving beguines still flourish. Surprisingly perhaps in countless sayings, beguines are associated with idleness and laziness: 'To work is beatific', the beguines said, 'and two of them carried a single bean stalk'. Or as the devil said, when walking between two beguines, 'I am the virtue in the middle',[2] and strange as it may seem – especially because history depicts their chastity – it is not uncommon, nowadays, to find brothels called 'beguinage' in Belgium. In the early days, the terminology 'the blue beguine' was a slang term for a prostitute.

Felix Timmermans (1886-1947), one of the most famous Flemish authors of the twentieth century immortalised the beguines in several works with highly evocative language: the *Begijnensproken* [*Beguinage Tales*, 1911], *De zeer schone uren van Juffrouw Symforosa, begijntje* [*The Very Beautiful Hours of Miss Symforosa, Beguine*, 1918] and in certain pages of *Schoon Lier* [*Beautiful Lier*, 1928].[3]

2. The examples are taken from K. C. PEETERS, *Eigen aard: Grepen uit de Vlaamsche folklore* (Antwerp, 1946), p. 143. Also A. DE COCK, 'Spreekwoorden en zegswijzen over de vrouwen, de liefde en het huwelijk: de begijn', *Volkskunde* 19 (1907-1908) 18-22.
3. In 1924, Timmermans also illuminated the *Begijnen sprookjes* [*Beguine Tales*] of Jozef Arras. Together with Antoon Thiry, he edited the *Begijnhofsproken* [*Beguinage Tales*] in the 1920s.

Typical of his style is the following passage of the last-named book, translated into English.

> The beguinage is the almond tree of Lier. And to con-serve the flavour and the scent well, it stands beside the River Nete under the fresh curtain of the beguine moat, straight in the stream of the fields, but enfolded and guarded by ivy-covered walls and bulky bolted gates. Behind them, under the festive turret, in the old houses, where in the night old memories creak on the stairs, the bright blossom of the pious beguine souls blooms. Silence and solitude slide over the pallid cobblestones along the white streets. There, the houses stand as if under water, as straight plants in a pond. Faith keeps everything white and quiet [ ] and out of the house, names, painted on the doors, murmur: 'The Vineyard of the Lord', 'the Sweet Name Jesus', 'Mount Tabor', 'The Flight to Egypt'. Silence is like oil; now and then, it gurgles up and then the bell chiming wells up out of the cake-like ajour turret. The white, silent streets, with here and there the Stations of the Cross stuck to the walls, are like the naive little scenes of Jesus's bitter suffering.[4]

This quotation indicates that the beguine movement was perceived to be over by the second half of the twentieth century, but the romanticised image of beguines lives on. Today, many beguinages (Dutch: *begijnhof,* or *begijnhoven* in the plural) are restored and activities such as taking wedding photographs, folk festivals and filming take place. This romanticism is

---

4. F. TIMMERMANS, *Schoon Lier* [Beautiful town of Lier], 2nd ed. (Amsterdam and Antwerp, *s.d.*), pp. 42-43.

in strong contrast with the beguine movement's initial purpose. The first beguines were not sweet-voiced and silly women, but strong and devout. They had to fight for recognition and autonomy in male-dominated times, where female independence and initiative was not appreciated. They succeeded, but history took its toll.

There are many historical records of the beguines in existence. In the early period, small groups of devout women lived scattered all over town. This can be verified by existing papal and episcopal documents, as well as in letters that beguine leaders wrote to 'kindred spirits', and in the decrees of councils still available in the archives. However, we still have to be careful with the earliest documentary sources, because some were used for propaganda. Later, when the beguines started living in community, we find in the beguinages even more documentation pertaining to the movement, such as statutes, beguine rules of conduct, literary works written by the beguines themselves, other devotional literature, correspondence from beguines to custodians and others, and writings by opponents.

In this synthetic study, we shall mainly examine monographs. From them we shall try to give an up-to-date *status quaestionis*. The main goal of this survey is to offer a well-supported synthesis. This, in contrast to the proliferation of different doubtful hypotheses on many subjects relating to the beguines, such as the origins of the movement, the etymology of the word 'beguine', the social status of the candidate beguines, the beguine mystics and the so-called revolutionary feminism of the first generations. This overview is written in English but drawing on secondary literature in many languages, since there are only three monographs on the beguines in English.[5]

In the opening chapter we sketch the historical context in which the movement emerged. We will mention certain key European developments in the twelfth century and subsequently give a more detailed approach of the spiritual developments of the same period. It is now clear that beguines were less original than was previously thought. Nevertheless they confounded their contemporaries when they developed the social status of semi-religious people. Also, their theological and mystical opinions were novel.

This historical chapter also offers a synthesis of the different stages of the beguine movement, dis-

5. D. PHILIPS, *Beguines in Medieval Strasburg: A Study of the Social Aspect of Beguine Life* (Palo Alto, 1941); E. MCDONNELL, *The Beguines and the Beghards in Medieval Culture: With Special Emphasis on the Belgian Scene* (New Brunswick, NJ, 1954) and S. VAN AERSCHOT & M. HEIRMAN, *Flemish Beguinages: World Heritage* (Leuven, 2001). Since the 1980s, activity and interest in the subject has grown in North America. A bibliographical overview of American publications can be found in J. E. ZIEGLER, 'Secular Canonesses as Antecedent of the Beguines in the Low Countries: An Introduction to Some Older Views', *Studies in Medieval and Renaissance History* 13 (1992) 117-135. There are almost no French and German publications.

tinguishing four stages in their medieval development. The beguinage courts that can now be visited in Belgium and the Netherlands (together with some other extant examples in northern France and northern Germany) were established during the last stage of that development. They are at the quiet and peaceful ending of an organisation that was once thought to be quite revolutionary.[6]

We shall also study the problems the first beguines encountered, and why they were doomed to disappear in most European countries. Early on in their history they were confronted with opposition, which would finally succeed in discrediting the organisation in the whole of Europe, apart from the Low Countries. The reason why they were able to persist in these areas is worthy of particular attention. Lastly we will deal with further developments of the beguine movement in the Low Countries during the sixteenth to twentieth centuries.

The second chapter examines the characteristic spirituality of the beguines, with particular attention to the works of Hadewijch. Beguines were best known for their 'mystic spirituality' and this was central to their self-identity. For this reason, we will refer to similar mystical prose and poetry written by medieval women.

6. Situation in France: McDonnell, *The Beguines and the Beghards*, pp. 224-233.

The third chapter deals with beguinage architecture, the organisation and daily life within the court. The final chapter introduces the thirteen Flemish beguinage that were recently granted World Heritage status.

| I |
HISTORICAL BACKGROUND

| 1 | Introduction to the Twelfth Century

Frequently the Middle Ages have been considered an obscure, even savage period, but looking more closely at the twelfth century, we can easily show this to be wrong. The twelfth century had its share of political and military problems: the crusades were at their height of success with the taking of Acre in 1104. In 1125, the conflict between the German Welf (or Guelph) and Ghibelline dynasties started as part of the protracted struggle for political supremacy between the pope in Rome and the Holy Roman emperor. In mid-century England, civil war raged as by-product of the dynastic struggles over Norman and Angevin territories. By 1148, the Second Crusade ended, having failed to capture Damascus, and in 1187 Saladin conquered Jerusalem.

Some well-known monarchs reigned in the twelfth century, such as Friedrich I Barbarossa, who ascended to the throne of the Holy Roman Empire in 1155 at the age of thirty-two. He reigned for thirty-five years. In 1167, the year in which Genghis Khan was born, Barbarossa occupied Rome and overthrew Pope Alexander III. In 1180, the new king of France, the other principal Western European power, was the equally significant Philippe II Auguste. At this period in England, Eleanor of Aquitaine was inciting her two sons Richard the Lionheart and King John to revolt against their father, Henry II. The revolt turned out to be unsuccessful, but it loosened England's political influence within and her ties to France.

Notwithstanding these instances of political and military turmoil, the twelfth century was a prosperous period. Everywhere in Europe population figures were rising, which was particularly reflected in the foundation of new towns, the granting of charters for new market-towns, and the development of large, international trading cities. Moreover the colonisation of East-Central and Eastern Europe by Germanic-speaking peoples started in earnest.

In the religious sphere we may note the following. During the ninth and tenth centuries secular lords and monarchs assimilated increasing ecclesiastical power, particularly in their control of monasteries and dioceses in former mission-areas, such as Germany. After the Investiture Struggle, which was concluded in 1122 by the Concordat of Worms, the ecclesiastical authorities had regained supremacy. Papal authority reached a peak during the reigns of Pope Alexander III (1159-1181) and Innocent III (1198-1216).

During this century the resurgence of monastic life was breathtaking. In France Robert of Molesme (d. 1111) founded the Cistercian Abbey of Clairvaux

in 1097 and Bernard of Clairvaux (1090-1153) popularised the order so much that it soon contained 80
monasteries and 66 nunneries. Bernard's name will
crop up later, when we examine the spiritual reforms
he started. Around the same time, in 1162, in England,
Thomas Becket became archbishop of Canterbury
in 1162. Soon after his murder in 1170 Canterbury
joined Santiago and Cologne as one of Europe's most
important pilgrimage sites.

In understanding the beguine movement, urbanisation is of special importance. Burghers increasingly
united to promote their own interests against those
of their lord, secular or ecclesiastical, and to regain
influence in local government. In so doing small communities like medieval towns were able to take a lead
in commercial and economic life and even play an
important role in international trade. Towns became
more and more important for the economic life of
their hinterlands.

This vernacularisation of society was paralleled by
the gradual use of vernacular languages instead of
Latin in social and cultural communication. Priests,
such as Otto of Freising (ca. 1111/14-1158), William
of Malmesbury (ca. 1090-ca. 1143) and Saxo Gram-
maticus (d. ca. 1220), still recorded historical facts
in Latin, but gradually the vernacular was becoming the language of poetry and prose. In France, the
chanson de geste, an idealising genre of epic poetry
loosely based on historical episodes, was becoming
popular. Perhaps the most famous examples are the

Chanson de Roland and the cycle about Charlemagne. Such epic poems became widely spread in England, the Holy Roman Empire and the Low Countries. More popular still were the late-twelfth-century author, Chrétien de Troyes's chivalric epics on Arthurian topics and the Holy Grail, the so-called *chansons de geste* and his German-speaking compatriots, Walther von der Vogelweide (d. ca. 1230), Hendrik van Veldeke (d. ca. 1190) and Hartmann von Aue (d. ca. 1215).

France, more particularly the Ile-de-France, was the home for artistic advances in architecture which would influence western Europe to the present day. Abbot Suger (ca. 1081-1151) started in 1132 to develop vast building-plans for an abbey in Saint Denis, just north of Paris, which would be the originator of the Gothic style. Contrary to Romanesque architectonics height, space and light became the in-words. Heavy support-walls disappeared and were replaced by light, lofty pillars holding the roof. This made room for more, and larger, windows. Such construction was made technically possible by the introduction of external flying-buttresses and better load-bearing pointed arches and cross-ribbed vaults between the pillars. The outside decoration with sculptural work was equally flamboyant, and inside, multi-coloured biblical scenes, animals and plants were depicted on the walls.

This period is also known as the Twelfth-Century Renaissance, due to the advances in educational and intellectual life. Education, at that time, was frequently organised within monasteries and other religious institutions (such as cathedrals), among which perhaps the school at Chartres was the best known.[1] In the twelfth century scholarship emphasised precision, clarification and dissection of terms; this characteristic method of analysis is what we now call 'scholasticism'. Subsequent scholasticism was rooted in the work of theologians such as Anselm of Canterbury (d. 1109), Hugh of Saint Victor (d. 1141) and Peter Lombard (d. 1160). People were optimistic about the abilities of human reason, no doubt underpinned by the wider socio-economic situation, with a growing population, a prosperous economy, and the growth of towns and cities. Urban theological schools flourished in this environment.

The new *scolares* challenged the grammarians and logicians of the cathedral schools of Chartres and Laon.

1. At Chartres Neoplatonism emphasised the duality of body and soul and the distinction between material and the spiritual was accentuated. In the twelfth century, scholars like William of Conches, Adelard of Bath, Bernard of Chartres, Peter Abelard and others studied that contrast. Joined together at Chartres, they were radical *moderni*, basing their ideas on physical, rather than on metaphysical, evidence. See further, A. BAUER, *Vézelay: Een verhaal van vrijheid en macht* (Kapellen, 1997[2]), pp.86-89. See also L. C. MacKINNEY, *Bishop Fulbert and Education at the School of Chartres*, Texts and Studies in the History of Mediaeval Education, 6 (Notre Dame, IN, 1957).

They developed the *quaestio*, a formal method for reasoning, questioning existing theses, and proposing new positions.[2] They used the same determination and urge for clarity in conceiving theological constructions as had been done in building Gothic cathedrals. By 1200 these first *scolares* and *magistri* formed their own interest groups, or guilds (*'universitates studiorum'*), alongside other urban 'universitates' of craftsmen, or guilds. Thus were formed the leading centres of study at Paris, Oxford, Salerno and Bologna.[3] At the same time, a large number of translations of ancient Greek writings led to a revived interest in the classics.

| 2 | Spiritual Revival

Many authors explain the origin of the beguine movement by referring only to the changing spiritual climate. But religion is part of broader culture, hence our discussion here of the broader cultural changes in the twelfth century. It is impossible to say what had precisely caused these changes, so we will examine the changes in spiritual life also in relation to changes in political, socio-economic and cultural life.

Historians of mentalities locate the changing spiritual climate to the second half of the twelfth century.

---

2. M. D. CHENU, *La théologie au 12ᵉ siècle* (Paris, 1956), p. 329.
3. A recent and instructive book on this subject is J. LE GOFF, *Les intellectuels au Moyen Âge* (Paris, 1986²).

Together with the renewed interest in ancient learning, an increasingly secularised worldview liberated the outlooks of the laity.[4] The ties between the sacred and the profane were loosening. That was why laymen were able to unite themselves with greater autonomy from the ecclesiastical structures. The start of this process was the establishment of the first universities. From this period onwards intellectual activity was no longer centred in monastic cloisters.[5]

4. Art can reveal this process of increased secularisation. In Romanesque churches the sacred was separated from the earth/the material. In the Gothic era, statues were placed on the exterior of churches. The sacred gained, in its symbolic representation, a more sensual, worldly character. The distant sacred from earlier times was now represented more clearly. Holy Scripture was interpreted in a more human, pathetic dimension. The eucharistic reforms in this period were part of the same development, because the Church made it possible for believers to witness the mystery of the daily communion (BAUER, *Vézelay*, p. 84 and R. BAUER, J. DE VISSCHER, H. VANDEVONDELE & D. VAN DEN AUWEELE, *De twaalfde eeuw: Een breuklijn in onze beschaving* [Kapellen, 1984], pp. 105-107). On the eucharistic controversies: H. DE LUBAC, *Corpus mysticum: L'Eucharistie et l'Église au Moyen Âge: Étude historique*, Théologie, 3 (Paris, 1944).

5. We should not exaggerate the distinction medievals drew between the material and spiritual. Medieval dualism was not as sharp as it is for post-Enlightenment people: '[ ] la pensée médiévale ne connaît pas fondamentalement la division moderne qui découpe matérialisme et spiritualité' in A. DE LA CROIX, *L'érotisme au Moyen Âge: Le corps, le désir et l'amour* (Paris, 1999), p. 101.

Theology was influenced by this securalisation and vernacularisation, but in turn shaped it, assisting for instance the emergence of religious movements for the laity, such as the beguine movement. For example, scholars at Chartres claimed between 1120 and 1140 that after the creation of the universe God withdrew himself from direct involvement and human beings should submit to the laws of the universe.[6] Bernard of Clairvaux put that theology in practice by developing a way towards the *perfectio christiana* for noblemen in military orders such as Knight's Templars and Hospitallers ('Knights of Malta').

Some historians claim that 'individualism' and 'humanism' originated in the twelfth century. Here, the term 'individualism' should be understood as a more personal approach to the human being in connection to God and others. If earlier Christians focused on the salvation of the entire Church and how to achieve this, later they focused more on the salvation of the individual person and on its achievement. Humanism emerges after the increasing faith in human abilities, in particular, one's rational abilities. These developments were especially noticed in monastic life, but they also influenced the world outside the cloister. Without

---

6.   A. VAUCHEZ, *La spiritualité du Moyen Âge occidental (8ᵉ-13ᵉ siècle)* (Paris, 1994²), pp. 71-72.

these developments the beguine movement would have been inconceivable.[7]

At an institutional level, the Church had been undergoing what is now termed the Gregorian Reform. The reform was named after its initiator, Pope Gregory VII (1073-1085), the former monk Hildebrand. But it had its roots in the previous curia of Leo IX. Under the papacy of Leo IX, Hildebrand's influence had been increasing and the people whom attended Pope Alexander II's funeral, elected Hildebrand Pope. During his papacy, many reforms were carried through to prevent secular lords from influencing ecclesiastical appointments and ensuring that there were no dynastic or familial links that diverted a cleric's loyalty from the Church hierarchy. Thus, they focused on banning simony (buying of offices), imposing clerical celibacy and preventing lay rulers or lords making any clerical appointments. The Church became more and more independent from the secular authorities and consequently

7. An elaborated study on the changing mentality in this period is L. DUPRÉ, *Passage to Modernity: An Essay in the Hermeneutics of Nature and Culture* (New Haven, CT, 1993). E. KINGMA, *De mooiste onder de vrouwen: Een onderzoek naar religieuze idealen in twaalfde-eeuwse commentaren op het Hooglied* (Hilversum, 1993), pp. 36-37. Also I. VAN 'T SPIJKER, 'De ordening van affecten: kloosterleven in de twaalfde eeuw', R. E. V. STUIP & C.VELLEKOOP, *Emoties in de Middeleeuwen* (Hilversum, 1998), pp. 115-134.

became the supreme authority of the religious community.[8] The Gregorian Reform laid the foundation for the renewal of monastic life, introduced some solutions to the problem of pastoral care in villages, towns and cities, and led to the rebirth of apostolic life.

Since the second half of the eleventh century another spiritual change in people's mentality had been taking place. People wanted to go back to basics, which involved the original sources. In the field of culture, people wanted to study the original texts by Latin writers such as Cicero and Virgil. In Church life, there was a return towards the early ideal of the *ecclesia primitiva*, as described in Scripture or as proclaimed by the Church Fathers. The ideal was the *vita apostolica*, the earliest Christian way of life as depicted in the Acts of the Apostles. In monastic life, this caused a renewed interest in an ascetic way of life. Many monks left the monasteries in order to live a hermit's life in total isolation, following the precedent of the early Desert Fathers. Inside the monastic court, the monastic rules were more strictly obeyed and interpreted. First Cluny and its daughter-houses tried

8.   Because the Church wanted to separate itself from lay influences, the popes believed that emperors and kings had to acknowledge papal supremacy. But this led the Church to develop its own counterbalancing secular structure and made it increasingly appear worldly (BAUER, *Vézelay*, p. 91).

to live up to the Rule of Benedict more strictly. Later, Cîteaux and others attempted an even purer form.[9]

The eremitic life is linked to beguinism. Hermits were an integral feature of Celtic Christianity which, via the Anglo-Saxon missionaries across the Rhine and within the Low Countries, proved a great legacy in these lands. In the Low Countries people revered the model lives of saints such as Bavon, Ghislain, Landrada, Amalberga, Landelin and Remacle. An abbot could for example, give permission to a monk to withdraw to the 'desert' for a particular period. In the twelfth century this option became very popular. Hermitism became more organised, though only one order has survived to the present day, namely the Carthusians, founded by St. Bruno between 1081 and 1084. In these eremitic movements the distinction between clergy and laity was transcended because both ordained and unordained people were part of the movement.[10] Another popular alternative for clergy with pastoral duties was to retreat from the isolation of parish life to live in community as 'canons' with other priests. In the Low Countries arguably the most significant order of regular canons was the Order of Prémontré, better known as Premonstratensians or

9. VAUCHEZ, *La spiritualité*, pp. 73-75.
10. *Ibid.*, pp. 82-86.

Norbertines, founded by Norbert of Gennep in 1120.[11] Also, one should also not forget the reformed congregations of the Benedictine Order, of which the Cistercians were the most successful.[12]

The growing impact of the ideal of poverty in everyday life is also evidenced by the fact that more and more lay persons were being canonised in this period, a tendency that was dramatically reversed in the late thirteenth century. Before the twelfth century it had been almost impossible for laymen to be canonised, except in the case of monarchs such as Stephen I of Hungary (ca. 969-1038) or Olaf II Haraldsson of Norway (995-1030) who enabled the conversions of their lands to Christianity. But by the beginning of the twelfth century, a total change in mentality had taken place, many nobles were still being canonised, not because of their rank, but rather because they lived up to the ideal of poverty. Elisabeth of Hungary (ca. 1293-1336) was praised because of the charity she showed towards the poor and the

---

11. R. BOUDENS, *De kerk in België: Momentopnamen* (Averbode, 1994), pp. 39-42. F. PETIT, *La spiritualité des Prémontrés aux 12ᵉ et 13ᵉ siècles* (Paris, 1947) and S. WEINFURTER, 'Der Prämonstratenser im 12. Jahrhundert', M. MÜLLER, *Marchtal* (Ulm, 1992) 13-30.
12. BOUDENS, *De kerk in België*, pp. 38-39. L. J. LEKAI, *The Cistercians: Ideals and Reality* (Kent, 1977) and B. K. LACKNER, *The Eleventh-Century Background of Cîteaux* (Washington, DC, 1972).

homeless.[13] This development of the *vita apostolica* became embedded in mainstream Christianity through the mendicant orders which emerged in the thirteenth century. Their success also roused the conscience of the wealthy to have pity on the *nihil habentes*.[14]

| 3 | The Cultural and Religious Settings

Up to now we have discussed the institutional framework in which the beguine movement occurred, but another important aspect is to understand why the beguines became mainly established in the Low Countries and why a sister-movement of earlier beguines in Southern France died out. To understand the French situation, we need to reflect on the link

13. VAUCHEZ, *La spiritualité*, pp. 154-157. Vauchez counts ten canonisation procedures of women. Only four women saw the process through to canonisation, thanks to their devote confessors. They are all women remarkable for Christian charity and penance: Hedvig of Andechs (Silesia) (d. 1243), Elisabeth of Hungary (d. 1231), Rosa da Viterbo (d. 1253) and Angela da Foligno (d. 1309). The list was later filled up with women who challenged the Church: Birgitta of Sweden (d. 1373) and Catherine of Siena (d. 1380). See A. VAUCHEZ, *La sainteté en Occident aux derniers siècles du Moyen Âge* (Paris and Rome, 1981), pp. 402-410 and 427-448.

14. M. MOLLAT, *Les pauvres au Moyen Âge* (Paris, 1974), pp. 147-165.

between the Occitan troubadours and their concept of courtly love (so characteristic of their lyric style), the dominance of affective love in mainstream theology of the late eleventh century, and the simultaneously growing spiritual force, encaptured in a yearning towards a return to the *vita apostolica*.[15]

In Aquitaine, a large area with hills and plateaux in the South-West of France, of which Bordeaux was the capital, the first troubadours emerged. The best known troubadours were Pierre Vidal (d. 1204), Bernard de Ventadorn (b. 1125), Jaufre Rudel (b. ca. 1150) and Rambaut de Vaqueiras (d. 1207). They were wandering singers who sung in the vernacular *langue d'oc*. They were called troubadours because they wrote both the lyrics and the accompanying melodies themselves (*trouver*). The *canso* was a type of love poem that consists of several stanzas written according to a particular rhyme pattern. The troubadours promoted the idea of *fin amors* in their poems. In Western Europe, this was a new way of seeing love. Opposing the prevailing pragmatism of imposed marriage or seduction, *fin amors* idealised a personal relationship in which the woman was master and the man took the role of a vassal. The term *maitresse* is the original word which refers to rules of courting

---

15. P. MOMMAERS, *Hadewijch: Writer, Beguine, Love Mystic* (Leuven, 2004), pp. 25-33. See also the introduction of C. HART, *Hadewijch: The Complete Works* (New York, 1980).

or customs of civility between men and women which are still practised today.

The origins of the troubadour lyric lay in a fundamental paradox. Real love was not about possessing the beloved, *amer per aver*, but about *amor de lonh*, distant adoration, a state that would keep *desire* alive. In *Lanqan li jorn*, Jaufre Rudel sings 'Ja mais d'amor no'm jauzirai / Si no'm jau d'est amor de lonh', which roughly translated means: 'I cannot enjoy any love, but distant love'.[16] In the twelfth century, *fin amors* denoted a civilised controlling of one's temper, emotions and urges, refinement of one's speech and looks, respect for women and austerity. Hence it would certainly be wrong to reduce the word 'courtliness' only to courtly love, even though courtly love had an important impact on the renewal of contemporary spiritual life.[17]

16. The text can be found on CD HMX 2901524.27: *Troubadours / Cantigas de Maria*, executed by the Clemencic Consort under the guidance of René Clemencic. Speaking of music: music of beguinages can be found on the CD *Zingen en spelen in Vlaamse steden en begijnhoven/ Music in Flemish Cities and Beguinages* (CD Eufoda 1266). Also Hadewijch's music becomes popular. Examples of books with CD's included: *Hadewijch: Die minne es al* (Leuven, 2002) and *Ende Hier Omme Swighic Sachte* (Amsterdam, 2002).
17. J. JANSSENS & C. MATHEEUWSEN, *Renaissance in veelvoud: Als dwergen op de schouders van reuzen? (8ste-16de eeuw)* (Leuven, 1995), pp. 151-152 and F. X. NEWMAN, *The Meaning of Courtly Love* (New York, 1968).

In Christian spirituality this courtly language appeared in the mystical works of Bernard of Clairvaux.[18] His emotional language was not the result of any personal, ecstatic or visionary experience, but of a passionate reflection on religious experience, in particular mystical experience. His most important mystical works were the *Sermones supra Cantica Canticorum*, a collection of 86 sermons devoted to the Old Testament Song of Songs, chapters 1:1-3:1.[19] As with the new literary movement of courtly love, Bernard also emphasised emotions and experiences, *affectus* and *experientia*. Affection

---

18. Bernard owed much to, *inter alia*, Peter Damian (d. 1072).
19. U. KÖPF, 'Bernard de Clairvaux', P. DINZELBACHER (ed.), *Dictionnaire de la mystique* (Turnhout, 1993), p. 101. Guillaume de Saint Thierry, a contemporary of Bernard and also a Benedictine monk, published an *Expositio super Cantica Canticorum*. With that book, he influenced the mystics of Brabant, for example the beguine Hadewijch. To him, the beginning of spiritual experience is faith and that is the reason why the believer always carries God with him. The ultimate perfection of faith happens in a deep knowledge of love and a mutual struggle in love between God and men (K. DUCHATELEZ, *Geschiedenis van de christelijke spiritualiteit: Zien hoe groot onze hoop is* [Averbode and Kampen, 1995], p. 165). Guillaume wanted to know God other than as an abstraction. *Amor ipse intellectus est*, because love alone is able to touch the divine being who transcends the intellect (G. EPINEY-BURGARD & E. ZUM BRUNN, *Femmes troubadours de Dieu* [Turnhout, 1988], p. 18).

denotes the internalised process of becoming conscious of experiences and emotions in human beings.[20] Mystical love would come to play an important role in the first decades of the beguine movement as can be seen in the writings of Hadewijch (ca. 1200-1269). The early beguines paid much attention to their heart, soul and the soul's essence, thanks at least indirectly to Bernard.[21]

It is this author's opinion that beguines professed this form of mysticism as a means of securing their own identity in opposition to other religious and spiritual movements and to claim ownership of their spirituality in a context where theology had been the sole business of men.

Together with the blossoming of affective love a revolution in religious life was taking place in France. This movement's ideas could be generalised as 'starting to live again as the apostles did': the *vita apostolica*. There were three striking features to this new movement: firstly, the new apostles had to be poor; secondly, they had to preach the Good News or Gospel; and last but not least, the unusual

20. BERNARD OF CLAIRVAUX, *Hij kusse mij met de kus van zijn mond: Preken 1-9 over het Hooglied*, Mystieke teksten en thema's, 14 (Kampen and Gent 1999), pp. 10-11. English edition: *Bernard of Clairvaux. Selected Works*, ed. G. R. EVANS, The Classics of Western Spirituality (New York/Mahwah, NJ, 1987).
21. MOMMAERS, *Hadewijch*, p. 60-64.

occurence of women playing a crucial part in most of those movements.

Robert d'Arbrissel (ca. 1050-1117) was one of the first practitioners of this particular expression of the *vita apostolica*.[22] The Breton clergyman gave up his career. After practising an ascetic hermit's existence he started preaching with profound conviction. Thousands of people converted, leaving all they had to follow him. His followers were not only of both sexes, but came from both the lower and upper classes of society. Robert's views on women were surprisingly novel. Firstly, he rejected the idea that in all women there exists a particular evil force, against which no preaching or mercy was effective. He recognised that women had full personal consciousness and that the Holy Spirit dwelt within their bodies. Secondly, he provided an innovative solution to the spiritual problem of the relationship between religious men and women. In his opinion, the enclosure of monks and nuns within monasteries was a bad situation that 'locked out danger'. His followers, both male and female, lived together under one roof and even slept in close prox-

22. He is certainly not the only innovator, but surely the most important. Other figures are St. Bernard de Thiron (d. 1117), Vitalis of Savigny (d. 1122), Girald de Salles (d. 1120), and Henry de Lausanne (d. after 1145). On the *vita apostolica*, see chapter 2 of K. L. JANSEN, *The Making of the Magdalen: Preaching and Popular Devotion in the Later Middle Ages* (Princeton, NJ, 2001) and MCDONNELL, *The Beguines and the Beghards*, pp. 141-153.

imity to each other. And finally, by drawing women away from isolation within marriage he challenged the social centrality of marriage. Roscelline wrote to Abelard. 'I saw that the women in Sir Robert's religious movement flee away from their husbands, and that their husbands attempted to re-secure them'. Here lay the seed of a conflict that would haunt the beguine movement a century later.[23]

In the eleventh and twelfth centuries matrimony had become communalised and institutionalised as a sacrament.[24] This reinforced familial authority. It was because of this that the bride's father or guardian had to close the engagement and turn her over to the groom on the wedding day.[25] The Church tried to ensure the individuals' consent but in a feudal society the woman always had the weakest position.[26]

23. See the following monograph: J. DALARUN, *Robert d'Arbrissel, fondateur de Fontevraud* (Paris, 1986). We have quoted MOMMAERS, *Hadewijch*, pp. 14-18.
24. J. JANSSENS, *De middeleeuwen zijn anders* (Leuven, 1993), pp. 110-114. W. MOLINSKI, *Theologie der Ehe in der Geschichte*, Der Christ in der Welt. Reihe 7: Die Zeichen des Heils, 7a/b (Aschaffenburg, 1976).
25. V. VAN GOOL, 'Huwelijk', L. BRINKHOF, G. C. LAUDY, A. VERHEUL, & A. VISMANS (eds.), *Liturgisch woordenboek* (Roermond and Maaseik, 1962), part 4, pp. 1024-1025 and M. GREILSAMMER, *L'envers du tableau: Mariage et maternité en Flandre médiévale* (Paris, 1990).
26. P. L'HERMITE-LECLERCQ, 'L'ordre féodal (11e-12e siècles)', G. DUBY and M. PERROT, *Histoire des femmes en Occident. 2: Le Moyen Âge* (Paris, 1991), pp. 217-260.

Today, historians have strong contrasting opinions on women and their position in the society of that era. Some defend a positive image (R. Pernoud, R. Fossier), while others stress the suppression of women (G. Duby, J. Le Goff, D. Herlihy, P. L'Hermite-Leclercq). Yet Régine Pernoud argues that certain women held positions of power and were intellectuals.[27] Also, we often tend to forget that many women were traders, physicians, teachers and artists.[28] A study of Frankfurt has shown that women held 201 different occupations in that city.[29] Furthermore, an examination of archives in Lyon shows that in the Middle Ages just as many women were engaged in criminal activities as it is the case today.[30]

Robert d'Arbrissel's movement altered character around 1100 after the synod of Poitiers when Robert started to lodge his disciples in monasteries, instead of letting them wander about the cities. But here too

27. See R. PERNOUD, *Pour en finir avec le Moyen Âge* (Paris, 1977) and IDEM, *Lumière du Moyen Âge* (Paris, 1981). Pernoud gives examples of women who participated in the crusades, for instance Eléanore d'Aquitaine: R. PERNOUD, *La femme au temps des croisades* (*s.l.*, 1990).
28. H. MARTIN, *Mentalités médiévales (10ᵉ-15ᵉ siècle)* (Paris, 1996), pp. 421-422.
29. Quoted in McDONNELL, *The Beguines and the Beghards*, p. 85.
30. N. GONTHIER, *Délinquence, justice et société dans le Lyonnais médiéval* (Paris, 1993), pp. 113-135.

he had his own original ideas. He built so-called double-monasteries, where men and women lived in
their own seperated wings. The women's superior-
ity was striking: both spiritual and material authority
lay in the hands of abbesses.

Meanwhile, it had become clear that Robert of
Arbrissel's religious women had gradually reached
a new status. They were not lower-class people who
rose in the social ladder by joining a religious movement:[31] from the outset, only upper-class people had
been recruited. Robert's religious women strictly followed the ideal of poverty. After a while they were
prevented from direct preaching, but continued their
missionary work. However, some of these religious
women became spiritual guides to clerics and continued their preaching through intermediaries.

In order to understand the decline of the beguine
movement outside the Low Countries, it is important
to realise that the ecclesiastical powers were hostile
towards many revivalist religious movements. To live
up to the ideal of poverty, some people even resorted
to violence to convince others that it was the spiritual
way to live. Several investigations by the Church were
instituted against Robert d'Arbrissel. The Norbertines

31. We have to be careful with that statement because we
    know only the social status of the most rich religious
    women. From c. 1330 onwards, we have sources point-
    ing to poorer members too (L. K. LITTLE, *Religious Poverty
    and the Profit Economy in Medieval Europe* [London, 1978],
    pp. 132-133).

(though not the Gilbertine order in England) ceased the practice of double-monasteries. The Norbertines would later take responsibility for the beguine movement and also took care of other hermits who stayed in their regions. Other religious movements also tried hard to secure new members,[32] and some of these new orders and movements caused conflicts within the Church, mainly because of their uncompromising views.

In the eleventh century the Church charged some of those movements with heresy and in the twelfth century the issue assumed dangerous proportions.[33] The main conflicts were with *Pauperi* of Lyon, the Bogomils in South-Eastern Europe (today's Bosnia)

32. H. LEYSER, *Hermits and the New Monasticism: A Study of Religious Communities in Western Europe, 1000-1150* (New York, 1984) and V. SEMPELS, 'Opkomst en bloei van het kluizenaarsleven in de 12de en 13de eeuw', *Collectanea Mechliniensia* 20 (1947) 361-365.
33. Two remarks on 'heresy'. First, in the twelfth century the term does not mean the same as now. Then, a 'heretic' could simply mean a dissenter. Secondly, a certain heresy can bear different characteristics in different regions and in one region the same heresy can sometimes slightly change its characteristics (L. J. M. PHILIPPEN, *Het ontstaan der begijnhoven: Een synthetische studie* [Antwerp, 1943], pp. 18-19). For other heresies see K. ELM, 'Beg(h)arden', *Lexikon des Mittelalters* (Munich and Zürich, 1977), vol. 1, col. 1789 and MCDONNELL, *The Beguines and the Beghards*, pp. 430-438.

and the Cathar *perfecti* in the south of France. This process led to the creation of the Inquisition in Languedoc, the preaching and conversion techniques of the Dominicans and the destruction of many of these heterodox movements.

| 4 | Origins and Growth of the Beguine Movement in the Low Countries

First Stage of Development

Around 1170 or 1190, women in the Duchy of Brabant and the principality of Liège became remarkably interested in leading an evangelical life.[34] Some women did not fit into the existing regime of the enclosed life and chose to live in isolation as hermits. Other women who disliked eremitical isolation tried to create new alternatives. Frequently, groups of reli-

34. We do not exactly know where the beguine movement originated (whether at Nivelles, Oignies-sur-Sambre, Liège or elsewhere). It was certainly in the principality of Liège where beguines are mentioned for the first time in 1173. In the same region and in the same period a particular devotion to the eucharistic also came into being. It is difficult to locate the first usages of the term in our sense, because the term 'beguine' was used in many different ways in those days. An overview in English: McDonnell, *The Beguines and the Beghards*, parts 1 and 2.

giously-dedicated women decided to live together. Some stayed in their family homes, while others either moved to hermit cells next to the church, or lived together with other women who had the same religious beliefs. Many moved into homes in towns, often situated near hospitals and leper colonies. Despite their different lodgings they still formed one spiritual community with a distinct character. All tried to live up to the ideal of poverty, they prayed ecstatically and had a devoted respect for the sacrament of the altar.

In documents dating from that time, they were referred to as *mulieres religiosae* [pious women], *virgines continentes* [pure virgins] or *beghinae* [beguines]. The expression *mulieres religiosae vulgariter beghinae dictae* [devout women, commonly known as beguines] could often be heard in that period.[35] Not only did they receive the name by living piously (pious women had

35. MOMMAERS, *Hadewijch*, p. 18. The group of Clare of Assisi started in a way that is comparable to the beguines. From 1212 till 1215 Clare and her companions led a kind of enclosed life that had not yet been recognised by the ecclesiastical authorities. The only difference – at first sight – is that this kind of communal living started later in Umbria than in the Low Countries (A. MENS, *Oorsprong en betekenis van de Nederlandse begijnen- en begardenbeweging* (Antwerp, 1947), pp. 305 and 309). But both movements are part of the same spiritual reawakening that characterised Western Europe then (A. VAN MIERLO, 'Losse beschouwingen over het ontstaan der begijnen- en begaardenbeweging', *Ons Geestelijk Erf* 23 [1949], pp. 125-

always existed in Christendom), the also were part of an unknown phenomenon. They did special religious exercises, had a mystical spirituality, led a humble life and wore distinct clothing. Yet they were not religious because they had only made a private promise.[36]

James of Vitry said about early beguine life: 'In the south of France the phenomenon existed too, but the women were despised and mistrusted there. Some of the *mulieres religiosae* were pious virgins, who [...] scorned carnal temptations out of love for Christ and refused to enjoy worldly abundance in order to go to heaven. With great difficulty they were able to support themselves by manual labour, unless their parents were wealthy enough to support them. Many of the others were aged women [*matronae*], who zealously saw to the purity of younger girls, and who taught them salutary lessons, with the hope that they would later choose a spiritual marriage with the 'Heavenly Bridegroom'. Others were widows [*viduae*], who served God by fasting, praying, crying and by

126). Helvétius has argued that the beguines took the mendicants as a model, but I would argue that both movements had a common earlier inspiration (A.-M. HELVÉTIUS, 'Les béguines: Des femmes dans la ville aux 13e et 14e siècles', E. GUBIN & J.-P. NANDRIN, *La ville et les femmes en Belgique: Histoire et Sociologie*, Publications des Facultés universitaires Saint-Louis. Travaux et recherches, 28 (Brussels, 1993), p. 31).

36. PHILIPPEN, *Het ontstaan der begijnhoven*, p. 8.

doing manual labour to support themselves. [...]
Some, on the other hand, were married women who,
despite their married life, served God and raised their
children in fear of the Lord. They also devoted their
lives to praying, lived in sexual continence and tried
to lead an angelic life [*sanctae mulieres in matrimo-
nio Domino servientes*]'.[37] They were the *beghinae
indisciplinatae in saeculo manentes*, who would later
develop into *beghinae disciplinatae.*[38]

On the Name 'Beguines'

So far, we have been discussing the first stage of the
beguine movement.[39] Three more stages will follow,
but first we should explore the etymology of the
word 'beguine'. As to the derivation of this name,
several explanations have been proposed, but none
of them are conclusive. At first contemporaries
claimed the word was a derivative of St. Begga, the
legendary seventh-century founder of the beguine
movement. But this explanation was ascribed to her
after the formation of the movement, so can be dis-
counted. It was normal in the Middle Ages for orders
or congregations to claim they were founded by a

37. *Ibid.*, p. 9.
38. A short overview of the first stage in English: VAN AER-
    SCHOT & HEIRMAN, *Flemish Beguinages*, pp. 21-23.
39. We follow the classical interpretation in four stages of
    L. J. M. PHILIPPEN, *De begijnhoven: Oorsprong, geschiede-
    nis, inrichting* (Antwerp, 1918), pp. 40-126.

famous saint. In the sixteenth century, when the first historical publications on the topic appear, Erycius Puteanus (1574-1646), a professor of the university of Leuven, advocated a noble foundress and ever since Begga is the accepted founding mother of the movement. As early as 1912 Joseph Greven showed that the beguine movement emerged *ohne Gründer und ohne Gründerin.*[40] Still, many movements took over the name of at least one of the founders. In the case of the beguines not only St. Begga, but also the Liège priest Lambert li Bègues (d. 1177), were named as possible founders, but no evidence supports anything other than that he was a supporter and defender of the movement.[41] Originally, 'beguine' was synonymous with *mulier religiosa.* The word is used to refer to recluses, lay sisters, women who remained in their own houses and sometimes

40. Quoted by PHILIPPEN, *Het ontstaan der begijnhoven*, p. 5. A short overview in English on this topic: VAN AERSCHOT & HEIRMAN, *Flemish Beguinages*, pp. 30-31.
41. A. MENS, 'L'Ombrie italienne et l'Ombrie brabançonne', *Études franciscaines (supplément)* 17 (1968) 18. The surname of Lambert is written as *Li Bègues* or variants thereof. The *Woordenboek der Nederlandsche Taal* ('s-Gravenhage and Leiden, 1898), II: 1-2, p. 868 prefers *Lambert dit le Bègue*. The theory that Lambert is the source of the word 'beguine' is based on outdated facts and has been superseded by J. GOOSSENS, *De kwestie Lambert li Bèges († 1177)* (Brussels, 1984). Since the thirteenth century, a legendary image of him as a well-known popular preacher came into being and in historiography, historians were deceived by

even to Cistercian sisters and other nuns, but it is true that *mulier religiosa* had a more neutral meaning than the word beguine.[42] Most languages had pejorative vernacular terms to describe pious women and these words later often took heretical undertones. Examples are *beguine* in the Low

legends that explain why many scholars accepted him as the founder of the movement. According to the *Van Dale etymologisch woordenboek* (Utrecht and Antwerp, 1989), p. 92, the derivation from Lambert is improbable. They prefer *begina* as the source. *Begina* is the basis for the French word *beige* which is the natural grey-brown colour of wool. This is identical to the simple uncoloured clothing worn by the Franciscans or Grey Friars. (The word *sufi* incidentally has the same roots.) MENS, *Oorsprong en betekenis*, p. 17, subscribes to that viewpoint. VAN MIERLO 'Losse beschouwingen', argued against this position. Another possibility is that the word is derived from the Middle Dutch word *begen*, 'to pray'. But there are doubts whether this word ever existed. It is not found in E. VERWIJS & J. VERDAM, *Middelnederlandsch handwoordenboek* ('s-Gravenhage, 1885), part 1. Two things are certain. First, beguines and beghards are terms that can be applied to all kinds of devote women and men in the twelfth and thirteenth centuries (VAN MIERLO, 'Losse beschouwingen', p. 145 and the extended research in PHILIPPEN, *De begijnhoven*, pp. 16-39). Secondly, we must conclude that there is no convincing and yet accepted etymological origin for the word.

42. The religious and economic ties between Cistercians and *mulieres religiosae* are so close that some people have argued that the beguine movement is an offshoot of Cîteaux (MCDONNELL, *The Beguines and the Beghards*, p. 170).

Countries, *papelarde* in France, *humiliata* in Lombardy or *coquenunne* in Germany.[43] The connotation with heresy was certainly not entirely wrong, because initially the beguine movement was looked at with suspicion.[44] It was definitely true that the word beguine, just like *mulier religiosa*, was used initially to refer to both orthodox and heterodox women and also to laywomen, semi-religious people and nuns. This term applied to all pious women.[45] But from about 1250, however, the word was used to refer specifically to what we understand as beguines.

Stage Two of Development

Let us continue with the second phase in the movement's rapid expansion.[46] We often read that the beguine movement only emerged because there had been an increase in the female population during that period. After all, many men had died in crusades and other warfare, but no empirical correlation can

---

43. PHILIPPEN, *Het ontstaan der begijnhoven*, p. 11.
44. One can find some examples of that stream of abuses in S. AXTERS, *Geschiedenis van de vroomheid in de Nederlanden* (Antwerp, 1950), part 1, pp. 311-312.
45. VAN MIERLO, 'Losse beschouwingen', p. 145.
46. Short overview in English: VAN AERSCHOT & HEIRMAN, *Flemish Beguinages*, p. 24: Grouping of the beguines.

be shown.[47] Nor does it explain the formation of the 'beghard' movement, the male counterpart of beguines, and the simultaneous popularity of other religious movements (of men). The more significant demographic factor is the correlation between the beguines and the growth of towns. The most important grounds for the quick expansion of beguines were the renewed interest in the *vita apostolica*, the suppression of double monasteries and the strengthening of female autonomy. Scholars have accounted for the development of the beguine movement citing anything from socio-economic to religious reasons.[48] In our opinion there cannot be a one-dimensional explanation, but we wish to underline the general spiritual revival of this period.[49] Nowadays it is too easy to give socio-economic explanations, and they are insufficient to account for the religious revival during that period.

47. Historians and demographers still debate the question whether there was indeed a surplus of women. The main reason for the fight is a lack of demographic sources concerning population figures. See G. KOCH, *Frauenfrage und Ketzertum im Mittelalter: Die Frauenbewegung im Rahmen des Katharismus und des Waldensertums und ihre sozialen Wurzeln (12.-14. Jahrhundert)* (Berlin, 1962).
48. An overview of the literature on that subject is footnote 20 in HELVÉTIUS, 'Les béguines', pp. 23-24.
49. Even in the fourteenth and fifteenth centuries, when beguinages were founded especially for socially poor beguines (*domus pauperum*), religious motives still played the central part. See MCDONNELL, *The Beguines and the Beghards*, p. 88.

There was indeed a surplus of women, but for a different reason. We already said that matrimony had changed in the twelfth century. This meant in concrete terms that from then monogamy and marriage at the age of majority would be observed strictly and marriages with relatives or clerics would be prohibited. These measures created a surplus of marriageable women. Meanwhile, landowners wanted to secure their possessions acquired over many generations and not to subdivide their inheritance, which disadvantaged younger sons and reduced the marital opportunities for daughters, particularly when marriage involved an often sizeable dowry. As a result, many parents would have encouraged their daughters to enter a convent or something similar. When the beguine movement started, many of the early beguines were born in wealthy families, which supports the previous statement. Two groups of noble women increasingly looked for alternatives to marriage. They were either virgins who lacked the money to afford a dowry, or young women who could not remarry because of the principle of monogamy. We can also mention a third, rather small category of women who had decided to leave their husband or who had been left themselves. Their sole solution lay in a religious life.[50]

50. B. L. VENARDE, *Women's Monasticism and Medieval Society: Nunneries in France and England (890-1215)* (Ithaca, NJ, 1997), pp. 92-95. That statement is confirmed by a cartulary of Gent, quoted in L. J. M. PHILIPPEN, 'Begijnhoven

This change in marriage practice explains in more satisfactory terms the sudden success of religious movements of women in the twelfth century. Hugues de Grenoble's *vita*, from the twelfth century, mentions a shortage of convents so that not all the women could be housed.[51] Because traditional orders started to close their doors to women rather than to take them in, there was need for an alternative. Some women settled near convents, which was the case at Averbode, Tongerlo and Oignies[52]. This could be seen as the start of the beguine movement, though there was an important difference. The true movement mainly took place in the towns.[53] A second impetus for the search of a particular *modus vivendi* was the prohibition by the Fourth Lateran Council (1215) to

en spiritualiteit', *Ons Geestelijk Erf* 3 (1929) 168-169. In Flanders, many beguinages were founded because lots of women could not marry appropriately or did not have enough money to enter a convent. The religious authorities did not want those devote women to beg and so they found beguinages, where they could live with or without vows.

51. B. L. VENARDE, *Women's Monasticism*, p. 87.

52. AXTERS, *Geschiedenis van de vroomheid in de Nederlanden*, pp. 309-310. On the beguinage of Oignies: J. FICHEFET, *Histoire du prieuré de l'église Saint-Nicolas et du béguinage d'Oignies* (Aiseau, 1977).

53. The first beguines were located in cities and from 1240 in smaller towns. From about 1320 beguines are also found in rural areas (A. WILTS, *Beginen im Bodenseeraum* [Sigmaringen, 1994], pp. 40-41).

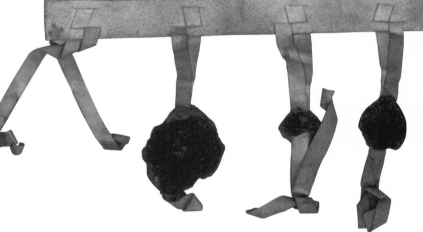

1. Leuven. Foundation charter of the Great Beguinage
(Leuven, Stadsarchief, Inv. Cuv. 4623)

2. Leuven. Gravestone of a beguine (fifteenth c.)

3. Diest. Portrait of Nicholas Esschius (1507-1578),
beguine pastor and reformer

4. Lier. Baroque entrance with the patron saint
of the beguines (c. 1690) (photo c. 1930)

5. Brugge. Dereliction of the beguinage
(early twentieth century)

6. Gent. Small Beguinage (c. 1930)

7. Herentals. Beguinage (c. 1950)

8. Gent. Entrance door to a convent
in the Small Beguinage

establish new orders or forms of monastic life that were not based on traditional monastic rules approved by the church.[54] That rule was repeated by the Synod of Lyon (1274). In spite of this rule, the beguines tried to escape the restriction by creating an alternative.

During the thirteenth century it therefore became unavoidable for the beguines to become enclosed and regularised. The challenge was to link *beghinae singulariter in saeculo manentes* [beguines living alone] with *beghinae disciplinatae* operating under obedience to the Church. To prevent the possibility of heresy it was decided to gather beguines into monastic-type structures. *Congregationes beghinarum disciplinatarum* [congregations of ordained beguines] came into being, free associations of laywomen who wanted a *conversio* [profession]. The beguines still lived separately as had been the case in the past, but they were now all to follow a certain prescribed rule and wear the same clothing. To outsiders they were beguines, but they called themselves *sorores* [sisters]. They were disciplined, which meant that they obeyed a *magistra* [mistress] and a set of rules. The previously mentioned Hadewijch appears to have been such a *magistra* of the beguines in Antwerp. During this second phase of the development of the beguine movement we see the gradual disappearance of

54. MENS, *Oorsprong en betekenis*, p. 277.

beguines who lived alone and not under the authority of the *magistra*. One result was that overall power
lay in the hands of local secular authorities.[55]

Stage Three of Development

The *congregationes* of this second stage of development were founded in imitation of other free
associations, such as pseudo-mystic and anti-sacer-
dotal movements. During the third stage they would
become more firmly organised, in order to deal with
defamatory accusations.[56] In the third stage, beguine
leaders also wished beguines to isolate themselves
from the outside world and live together in a shared
home under one roof in obedience to their mistress,
whilst being mutually supportive. In a still later development beguines moved into a convent and they
acquired the name *beghinae clausae* [enclosed
beguines]. Such a convent was called a *curtis* [court]
or *béguinage* [beguinage]. It had almost the same structure as a conventional nunnery. In 1215, the Lateran
Council had decided to curtail the establishment of
new orders. This was why in about 1216 John of Lier
and James of Vitry travelled to Rome to defend the
beguine movement, and they managed to secure ver-

55. MOMMAERS, *Hadewijch*, pp. 19-21 and PHILIPPEN, *Het
ontstaan der begijnhoven*, pp. 42-46.
56. PHILIPPEN, *Het ontstaan der begijnhoven*, p. 39.

bal approval from Pope Honorius III, for 'pious women' (not only in the diocese of Liège, but also in France and Germany) to live in communal houses and encourage each other to 'do good by mutual exhortation'. In the southern Low Countries, the concept had been successful.[57] It was mentioned in 1238 that in Kortrijk some poor beguines lived together in a home that belonged to Dignard of Halle. In 1234 a canon granted a home to poor beguines in Tongeren. Since 1230 beguines had started to gather in Brussels to pray under a priest's supervision in the chapel of Our Lady of the Vineyard.[58] In that period there were four convents in the town of Huy and nineteen in the town of Liège. They were spread throughout the town.[59]

The Fourth Stage of Development

Between 1230 and 1250, the last stage of the original phase of development and expansion took place, but it was largely confined to the Low Countries. Once more, additional measures were taken to protect the

57. On the protection by the hierarchy: McDonnell, *The Beguines and the Beghards*, pp. 154-164.
58. A. D'Haenens, *Begijnhoven van België* (Brussels, 1979), p.19. Literature on Brussels: P. Bonenfant, 'Une fondation patricienne pour béguines à Bruxelles au 13ᵉ siècle', *Mélanges Georges Smets* (Brussels, 1952), pp. 91-104 ; M. Thibaut De Masieres, *Le béguinage de Bruxelles* (Brussels, 1930); J. Van Brimeu, 'Brussel had een klein begijnhof. Waar 90 vondelingen werden opgevoed', *Brusselse Post* 7 (1957) 1.
59. Philippen, *Het ontstaan der begijnhoven*, pp. 40-41.

women against heretical influences. In Flanders, most beguinage foundation charters contained the following expression *ne vulpes effodiant vineam Domini* [that the foxes will not destroy the vineyard of the Lord]. Not surprisingly, most of the enclosed beguinages were instigated by Dominicans, who were notorious for fighting fiercely against heretics.[60]

Convents were detached from their parishes and united as new beguine parishes. In towns, beguines were obliged by secular authorities and by the Church to join a beguinage [*curtes beginarum*]. These private domains had a large gateway with their own church and, apart from the many similarly-sized homes, a beguinage would comprise a hospital and cemetery and a vast area where sheets were bleached. Most beguine parishes were generally located outside the town walls and near a river, which was necessary for bleaching sheets. In many Belgian towns, such beguinages are still open to visitors today and thirteen have recently been recognised by UNESCO as World Heritage Sites.

The beguinage of Leuven was erected in 1230, that of Sint-Amandsberg in 1234, and those of Antwerp in 1240, Kortrijk in 1241, Bruges in 1245, Anderlecht[61]

60. On the rise of beguine townlets: VAN AERSCHOT & HEIRMAN, *Flemish Beguinages*, p. 26.
61. On Anderlecht: M. JACOBS, 'Het begijnhof van Anderlecht', *Gemeentekrediet van België* 32 (1979) 285-294 and J. LAVALLEYE, 'Le Béguinage d'Anderlecht', *Folklore Brabançon* 10 (1930-1931) 33-35.

and Diest in 1252, Sint-Truiden and Lier in 1258, Aarschot in 1259, Herentals[62] in 1266, Hoogstraten in 1280 and Dendermonde in 1288. The exact founding date of other beguinages (such as those of Aalst,[63] Diksmuide, Hasselt, Mechelen and Tongeren) remain

62. On Herentals: J. LAUWERYS, 'Zo zongen de begijntjes te Herentals ca.1800', *Volkskunde* 73 (1972) 193-249; F. PRIMS, *Onze Lieve Vrouw Besloten Hof ter Herentals*, Campinia Sacra, 3 (Antwerp, 1933); H. SELS, 'De geschiedenis van de Herentalse infirmerie op het Begijnhof tijdens de XVIIde en XVIIIde eeuw', *Historisch Jaarboek van Herentals* (1986) 65-94 and (1987) 81-120; J. VERELLEN, 'Oorkondenboek van het begijnhof te Herentals', *Bijdragen tot de Geschiedenis* 33 (1950) 54-63, 167-191 and 246-255, and 34 (1951) 122-131 and 177-187. M.-Th. VRIENS, *Het oud begijnhof van Herentals (ca.1260-1508)* [unpublished master's dissertation Katholieke Universiteit Leuven] (Leuven, 1968). In Aarschot, a large community of beghards existed (M. BRUSSELAERS, J.BREUGELMANS, F. VANHOOF, W. SCHROEVEN & Zr. LUTGARDIS, *In peys ende gestichticheyt: Geschiedkundige bijdragen over het convent van de Bogaarden, het Gasthuis en de kloosters van Sint-Niklaasberg en de Kapucijnen te Aarschot*, Bijdragen tot de geschiedenis van het Land van Aarschot, 13 (Aarschot, 2001).

63. On Aalst: E. SOENS, *Cartularium en renteboek van het begijnhof St. Katharina op den Zavel te Aalst* (Aalst, 1912); *Het seldtsaem ende wonderbaer leven van Joanna Dedemaecker eertijts Beggyntjen in 't Beggyn-hof van Aalst [ ] gemaeckt ende beschreven door wijlen den seer Eerw. Heer mijn H. Franciscus Van Schonenberg Canoninck ende Deken der Coll. Kercken van S. Marten tot Aalst* (Leuven, 1759).

unknown.[64] Most, however, date back to the thirteenth century, the movement's peak of popularity.
There were 94 beguinages in modern day Belgium
alone.[65]

In the last stage of development, many groups
decided to choose the equivalent of a mother supe-
rior to oversee their life in collective homes, which
developed into beguinages The head of a beguinage
was called a Great-mistress, who obeyed local statutes
drawn up by the bishop. Some of the mistresses lived
alone while others lived together, first without and
later with, a prescribed rule. The beguinages remind
us of a once revolutionary movement started by some
mystic women. But the buildings are possibly the
movement's only chance of survival in the future.

The Male Beghards

In 1220 a separate branch of men started to follow
the beguines' example. They were called *beghards*.[66]

---

64. On Diksmuide: M. CATTEEUW, *Het Begijnhof van
Diksmuide*, unpublished notes (*s.l.*, 1966).
65. BOUDENS, *De kerk in België*, p. 56.
66. Just as the origin of the word beguine is unclear so too the
etymological roots of the word beghard. It could be linked
to what is now in English '*beggar*'. To beg was an important characteristic of the group (F. VERACHTERT ed.,
Voorsale des hemels ofte het begijnhof in de XVII Provinciën
[Retie, 1973], p. 13). Just like the word *beguine, beghard*
was somewhat pejorative. *Begardie* and *bagaerdie* mean
hypocrisy in Middle Dutch (J. J. VAN DER VOORT-VAN DER

In Latin literature, they were referred to as *boni chris-tiani* or *boni homines*. The oldest beghard home in the Low Countries is situated in Diest and was erected somewhat before 1257. That of Sint-Truiden was founded thirteen years later in 1270. After this many were started: in Aarschot, Antwerp, Tournais,[67] Maastricht, Mechelen, Leuven, Zoutleeuw and else-where. A beghard community lived together in communal houses, but this did not lead to the build-ing of beghard enclosures. These men supported themselves by spinning and weaving wool or by copy-ing manuscripts.[68] Burghers could identify beghards by their dark clothing and because they lived in com-munities. Fundamentally they did not differ from the beguines, attempting to lead devout lives, supporting themselves by manual work, following set rules and having an ascetic lifestyle. The main difference between beghards and beguines was that beghards refused the supervision of clerics, which led many

KLEIJ, *Verdam Middelnederlandsch handwoordenboek: supplement* [Leiden and Antwerp, 1983], p. 48). General introduction to this phenomenon: K. ELM, *Beg(h)arden*, col. 1798 and MCDONNELL, *The Beguines and the Beghards*, pp. 246-265.

67. M. LAUWERS & W. SIMONS, *Béguins et béguines à Tournai au Bas Moyen Âge. Les communautés béguinales à Tournai du 13ᵉ au 15ᵉ siècle*, Tornacum: Études interdisciplinaires re-latives au patrimoine culturel tournasien, 3 (Tournai/ Louvain-la-Neuve, 1988).

68. BOUDENS, *De kerk in België*, p. 57.

towards heterodoxy. This tendency prevented the further spread of beghardism.[69] In 1311 many orthodox beghards were convicted of heresy together with beguines, but just like the beguines they did not completely die out and survived in the southern Low Countries.

Early Conflicts with the Church on Account of Beguine Beliefs and Practices

From its earliest days the Church has regarded all lay movements with suspicion. Two of the most radical spiritual writers in Dutch of the later Middle Ages, Hadewijch and Ruusbroec, showed that they were not heretical as they did not take extreme positions. But mystical spirituality based on a personal relationship with God and novel expressions of Christian living were always prone to the charge of heterodoxy. Sometimes the danger was not in the author or initial protagonist but with their less sophisticated followers. During the explosion of fervour of the twelfth century many movements suffered a later crackdown by the Church authorities. Hadewijch and Ruusbroec did not name names in their writings, but

69. McDONNELL, *The Beguines and the Beghards*, pp. 246-265. An extended study on the end of the beguine and beghard movements is J.-C. SCHMITT, *Mort d'une hérésie: l'église et les clercs face aux béguines et aux béghards du Rhin supérieur du XIVe au XVe siècle*, Civilisations et Sociétés, 56 (Paris, 1978).

even they regard many of these early movements as heretical in nature.[70]

The later twelfth century saw growing moves by the Church to stifle what they believed to be heretical elements of these new lay movements. The harshest treatment was developed for the Cathars and Apostolic Brethren.[71] Beguines were also caught by the earlier decrees condemning nuns who lived in private homes, particularly the recent canon 26 of the Second Lateral Council, titled *Ut sanctimoniales in privatis domiciliis non habitent*. In 1139, bishops complained about the fact that women, who considered themselves as nuns, were living together in private homes without following a monastic rule. This was condemned: *Hoc tamen inhonestum detestandumque flagitium ne ulterius fiat, omnimodis prohibemus, et sub poena anathematis interdicimus.*[72] Only the death

---

70. For Ruusbroec see: P. VERDEYEN, *Jan van Ruusbroec: Mystiek licht uit de Middeleeuwen* (Leuven, 1996²), pp. 19-22.

71. The Apostolic Brethren were similar to the Cathars. They existed in northern France, Flanders, Liège, Cologne and the Rhineland (MENS, *Oorsprong en betekenis*, p. 29). Cathars too were not restricted to Languedoc but some were also active in Liège in the twelfth century (VAN MIERLO, 'Losse beschouwingen', p. 249). In the German lands and the southern Low Countries we also find another active lay movement called the Brethren of the Free Spirit.

72. VENARDE, *Women's Monasticism*, pp. 87-88.

penalty was a worse punishment than anathema since it meant complete social exclusion. The women had to decide either to stay in the outside world or live by strict enclosure.

In the thirteenth century the Church encountered problems with Italian penitential fraternities which also started as lay movements and owed something to the original model of the mendicant orders, of which the flagellants were undoubtedly the best known. They did not follow a monastic rule, but followed their own programme which did not include vows. In the eyes of clerics the Italian *penitenti* and beguines had similarities in terms of their structures and autonomy. The Church attempted to control these movements in 1280 by bringing them under the auspices of the mendicant orders as lay, third (or Tertiary) orders. The then Dominican Prior General, Muño de Zamora, established the Dominican Tertiaries in 1286 and in 1289. The Franciscans did likewise. However, some laity resisted this and became schismatic.[73]

The beguines in Languedoc, in particular certain radical groups from Béziers and Narbonne, who kept resolutely apart from the clergy and third orders, came into conflict with the Church authorities. The Synod of Béziers (1299) condemned the movement because it was illegal, having been founded after 1215

---

73. VAUCHEZ, *La spiritualité*, pp. 152-154.

(against the decrees of Lateran IV) and not recognised by the Church.[74] Moreover, they were accused of predicting the end of the world and the coming of the Antichrist. They were also closely sympathetic to the Spiritual wing of the Franciscans (who argued for a rigorist retention of the Order's early ethos, rather than an accommodation to its popularity and the contemporary world). Pope John XXII condemned the Spirituals' position on absolute poverty in 1317. These beguines also got caught in the activities of the Inquisition operating in Languedoc and Northern Spain against heresy.[75]

Beguines and beghards elsewhere were influenced by these other movements, particularly that of absolute poverty. During the second half of the thirteenth century, the phenomenon was assuming vast dimensions in the archdioceses of Trier, Mainz and Cologne. In 1277, the Synod of Trier warned beguines who preached heresies in the streets and in squares to cease. Accusations against beguines accumulated because, though beguines were able to work, they refused to do so. Further, they prayed together, preached (sometimes heterodox teachings) and had secret meetings – all of which were practices clearly condemned since the Council of Lateran IV. At the

---

74. Other restrictions came from the synods of Mainz (1261), Eichstätt (1282) and Fritzlar (1295).
75. M. ERBSTÖSSER, *Ketzer im Mittelalter* (Leipzig, 1984), pp. 165-167.

beginning of the fourteenth century the local ecclesiastical authorities decided to examine these cases. In
1307, during an examination some beguines told the
Archbishop of Cologne, Henry of Virneburg, that they
stood above the law and that only they would get salvation. In Antwerp, William Cornelius Lehren
proclaimed that only the poor would be saved and that
it was a sin even to have dinner with rich people. In
1317, the Bishop of Strasbourg, John of Dürheim, convicted some beguines and their female disciples; one
was burned at the stake, the others were driven out
of town. In 1319 a beguine was put on trial in Prague
for refusing to take communion from a priest. In 1322
the teaching of some beguines in Cologne caused a
scandal. And in 1332, a group of beguines was ques-
tioned in Silesia because they were suspected of
spreading impudent teachings. In most fourteenth-cen-
tury German towns, there are cases of beguine and
beghard convictions.[76]

These local actions were supported by papal and
conciliar decrees. In 1311 at the Council of Vienne, Pope
Clement V (1305-1314) issued two crucial decrees. The
first, *Cum de quibusdam mulieribus,* was directed
against the beguine movement. All objections against
the movement were summed up: that they were not
nuns, they did not take a vow of obedience, nor part
with their possessions, did not belong to an order that
had been approved by the Holy See – yet, they still

76. *Ibid.*, pp. 168-203.

acted as nuns by wearing a habit, discussing theological issues and even preaching publicly. The decree
censured women 'commonly known as beguines',
even if it excluded those 'truly pious' beguines who
led a pious and repentant life in their homes. The second decree, the constitution *Ad nostrum qui*, affected
beghards and beguines in German countries. Eight
theses regarding their ideas, which resembled those
of the Free Spirit, were condemned: Here follows a
brief description of these false beliefs:[77]

> 1) In the present life, man is able to acquire such a high
> level and nature of perfection, that he becomes inwardly
> sinless and is no longer able to make progress in grace.
> For they say: if someone remains able to make progress,
> we can find someone who is more perfect than Christ
> himself.
> 2) When a person reaches a certain level of perfection,
> man does not need to fast or to pray, because then his
> sensuality will be so perfectly subjected to spirit and rea-
> son, that he is able to concede freely whatever he likes
> to the body.
> 3) Those who are in the aforesaid level of perfection and
> spirit of freedom, are neither subject to human obedi-
> ence, nor bound by ecclesiastical commands, because
> they assert: 'Where the Spirit of the Lord is, there is free-
> dom'. [2 Cor. 3:17]
> 4) In the present life, man can crave for final beatitude
> according to all levels of perfection, which he will obtain

---

77. H. DENZINGER & A. SCHÖNMETZER, *Enchiridion symbolorum,
definitionum et declarationum de rebus fidei et morum*
(Barcelona, Freiburg and Rome, 1991[37]), pp. 388-389.

in a beatific life.

5) Every intellectual nature is naturally beatified and the soul does not require the Light of the Glory which illuminates the soul to see God and to enjoy Him beatifically.

6) Practising in virtues is meant for imperfect people and the perfect soul will repudiate virtues.

7) Kissing a woman is a mortal sin, because nature does not incline to it; the carnal act on the contrary is not a sin, because nature inclines to it – especially when the person who kisses had been seduced.

8) During the elevation of the body of Jesus Christ, they are neither allowed to stand, nor to exhibit reverence, because they assert that it would be a sign of imperfection to reduce the purity and level of their contemplation so much to allow themselves to think of the administration of the sacrament of the Eucharist or of the passion of the humanity of Christ.

In the southern Netherlands, beghards and beguines continued to flourish, but not without difficulties. There had been troubles with their beliefs also, but these will be dealt with more fully in the next chapter. The early beguines were generally women who criticised the social order. They did this by living up to the ideal of poverty, even though they were originally from the upper-classes, and not the lower orders.[78] A life in poverty caused two issues, that of mendicancy (beg-

78. Sometimes it is said that the beguine movement grew out of resistance against early capitalism and the wealthy lifestyle of some people. One forgets then, that mystical life also flourished among people who could easily live from their material wealth if they wished to do so. In those

ging and the receipt of financial support) and that of profitable work. The first generation considered mendicancy as a religious symbol of poverty. Some would even turn it into a profession, which caused protest in the Church. Manual labour was the solution, but in the fourteenth century beguines were selling goods in competition with guilds and craftsmen, who protested strongly against the situation. Apart from this, spiritual life was changing in the fourteenth century. The emphasis was moving towards improving one's own perfection and those of fellow human beings, spiritual reading and meditation as in the *Devotio moderna* movement a century later.[79]

In the Low Countries, Beguines were able to survive partly due to the absence of high-profile reactions against them, but mainly because of some powerful and influential advocates. One of the first supporters who defended the *beghinae clausae* at the Papal Curia in Rome, was the Augustinian Canon James of Vitry (ca. 1160/70-1240). He eventually succeeded in his task. He had expected to meet Innocent III, but due to the sudden death of the latter had to deal with Pope Honorius III (1216-1227). Shortly after his

days, many cloisters were meant only for the rich! In 1285, Pope Honorius IV condemned this as unChristian, but in reality such convents continued until they were destroyed at the French Revolution (McDONNELL, *The Beguines and the Beghards*, pp. 89-90).

79. WILTS, *Beginen im Bodenseeraum*, pp. 263-264.

election, this pope recognised the movement.[80] Around 1240, the learned Franciscan Robert Grosseteste, Bishop of Lincoln, praised the beguines for their ability to be self-supportive.[81] Later, Pope John XXII (1316-1334) included some protective measures in his bulls *Ratio recta* (1318) and *Sacrosancta romana* (1319) aimed at counterbalancing the condemnations made against the beguines by the Council of Vienne.[82] In 1343, Pope Clement VI (1342-1352) issued the bull *Persones vacantes* in which he declared that the beguine movement in the Low Countries was a tolerated institution. The beguine way of life was caught between disapproval and support.[83]

Even during the seventeenth century, there were still some intercessors who favoured the movement, such as John Malderus (d. 1633), the Bishop of Antwerp. He said this: 'Though it is more meritorious to dedicate oneself to God by the solemn vows of obedience, poverty and chastity, Belgian women, in general, are nevertheless of such character, that they would rather prefer to carry out tasks in a free way than to carry them out bound by a vow. They would rather live in eternal chastity in an unconstrained way

80. Axters, *Geschiedenis van de vroomheid*, part 1, p. 315 and Mens, *Oorsprong en betekenis*, pp. 278-279.
81. H. Grundmann, *Religiöse Bewegungen im Mittelalter* (Hildesheim, 1961²), p. 322.
82. W. J. Kroon, *Begijnhoven in Holland en Zeeland gedurende de middeleeuwen* (Assen, 1981), pp. 16-18.
83. Philippen, 'Begijnhoven en spiritualiteit', pp. 172-173.

than out of commitment. They prefer simple and constant obedience above taking the vow of obedience. They consider it more preferable to combine the moderate usage of temporal goods with giving away possessions for charitable or religious ends, than to suddenly part with their goods and live in poverty for the rest of their lives out of sheer necessity. In summary, the merits of repeated free submission compensate for the rewards of binding vows'.[84]

| 5 | The Beguine Movement in the Low Countries after the Middle Ages

As a result of the sixteenth-century Reformation and its ensuing struggle, beguinages suffered and were harmed.[85] The northern provinces of the Low Countries adopted the Reforms whole-heartedly and most beguinages, other than those in Amsterdam[86]

---

84. Quoted in PHILIPPEN, *De begijnhoven*, pp. 140-141.
85. 'From Ideal to Security', VAN AERSCHOT & HEIRMAN, *Flemish Beguinages*, pp. 32-33.
86. On Amsterdam: J. C. VAN DEN AKKER, 'Geschiedenis van het begijnhof te Amsterdam', *De Katholiek* 49 (1866) 281-308; 50 (1866) 89-144 and 196-233, and 58 (1870) 303-328; I. H. VAN EEGHEN, *Vrouwenkloosters en begijnhof in Amsterdam van de 14de tot het eind van de 16de eeuw* (Amsterdam, 1941); H. J. ZANTKUYL, 'De 14de en 15de eeuwse huisjes (Begijnhof 23 en 24)', *Amstelodamum* 53 (1966) 179-187; IDEM, 'Een 14de eeuws huis op het Begijnhof', *Amstelodamum* 50 (1963) 113-120; IDEM, 'De beken op het Begijnhof', *Amstelodamum* 67 (1980) 75-82.

and Breda, disappeared. In the Southern regions, changes took place more slowly, but still many beguinages were plundered and burned down. Until today, we can see the consequences. Sometimes, only the churches of the beguinage date from the Middle Ages, while the actual houses have been rebuilt during the seventeenth or eighteenth centuries.

In the late sixteenth century, after the initial religious strife of the Reformation, a revival took place. Most beguinages shared the same problems as the whole Roman Church: ignorance, superstition and moral decay.[87] The Counter-Reformation encouraged all forms of religious life and re-established the beguinages and beguine life. Some educated and enthusiastic priests brought about what we might call the second establishment period of the beguinages. The best-known of these priests were Nicolaus Eschius (d. 1578) of the beguinage at Diest, Wilhelmus Michiels (d. 1609) of Tongeren and Frederick Lumnius (d. 1602) of Antwerp. Johannes Hauchinus, archbishop of Mechelen between 1589 and 1598, was called *Patriarcha beguinarum* and declared new statutes for his archdiocese in 1588. These

87. On the spiritual revival: VAN AERSCHOT & HEIRMAN, *Flemish Beguinages*, pp.36-37. General overview of this period: M. TROOSKENS, 'De begijnenbeweging in de Moderne Tijd (16de-18de eeuw)', M. WYNANTS (ed.), *Begijnen en begijnhoven* (Brussels, 1994), p. 27.

statutes served as a model for other beguinages.[88]
Beguinages were rebuilt and re-inhabited by
beguines. The remains of medieval homes made of

88. PHILIPPEN, 'Begijnhoven en spiritualiteit', pp. 182-186. On
the beguinage of Antwerp: *Cort Begryp van het
godtvruchtigh ende deughtsaem leven van Sr. Anna van
Schrieck, Beggyntie op het Beggyn-hof van Antwerpen,
ghestorven den 30. Meert 1688 [ ] Beschreven ende by een
vergaedert door A.R. ende Is. M., Beggyntiens van het selve
Hoff* (Antwerp, 1698) [re-edited by J. LAMBRECHTS, (Hasselt,
1880)]; E. GEUDENS, *L'ancien béguinage d'Anvers: Essai
de topographie, Bulletin de l'Académie royale d'Archéologie
de Belgique* (Antwerp, 1906); *750 Jaar St.-Elisabethgasthuis
Antwerpen: 1238-1988* (Antwerp, 1988); *Lettre de Mr l'Abbé
S. à Mlle G. Béguine d'Anvers sur l'origine et le progrès de
son institut* (Paris, 1731); W. A. OLYSLAGER, *750 jaar begijnen te Antwerpen* (Kapellen, 1990); A. PEETERS, *Het Oud
Begijnhof te Antwerpen (ca. 1246-1542)* [unpublished master's dissertation Katholieke Universiteit Leuven] (Leuven,
1972); L. J. M. PHILIPPEN, 'De beteekenis van het oprichten
van het Begijnhof te Antwerpen en in de volksrijke
Vlaamsche steden', *Tijdschrift voor Geschiedenis en
Folklore* 6 (1943) 61-78; IDEM, *Het ontstaan der begijnhoven*; IDEM, 'Een vijftal oorkonden betreffende de
Antwerpse begijnen', *Bijdragen tot de Geschiedenis* 14
(1931) 129-141; IDEM, *Het volksonderwijs in onze mid-
deleeuwsche steden, inzonderheid te Antwerpen (1200-1563)*
(Antwerp, 1920); F. PRIMS, 'De biddende orden te
Antwerpen', *Antwerpiensia* 19 (1948) 214-217; J. VAN BRA-
BANT, *Het archief van het begijnhof van Antwerpen:
Repertorium van inventarissen, synoptische lijsten en
regesten*, Oud Antwerps kerkarchief. Kapittelschriften, 16
(Antwerp, 1978); IDEM, *In het begijnhof van Antwerpen op
wandel en op bezoek* (Antwerp, 1979).

wattle and daub were replaced by brick-and-mortar ones. Eighty such homes were reconstructed in Leuven between 1624 and 1697.[89]

In the comparative calm of the seventeenth century, there was once again time for more intellectual activities. Most religious orders tried to trace their founders. It was a period of religious renewal and people wanted to explore religion more deeply. Recalling ancient traditions and shining religious examples fit well within that context. Beguines also tried to trace their founders; this led them to Lambert li Bègues and St. Begga. From the seventeenth century Begga was regarded as the foundress of the beguine movement. In iconography she is portrayed wearing three crowns connected to her supposed founding of the canons of Andenne, and the beguine and beghard movements. She is also symbolically portrayed as offering protection to beghards and beguines by taking them under her cloak.[90] The seventeenth century was the Golden Age of the beguine movement.[91]

89. D'HAENENS, *Begijnhoven van België*, p. 7.
90. TROOSKENS, 'De begijnenbeweging', pp. 34-36.
91. VAN AERSCHOT & HEIRMAN, *Flemish Beguinages*, pp. 40-41.

In the eighteenth century, growth in the beguine movement stagnated and in some cases even declined. The number of vocations fell dramatically and beguinages ceased to expand. In Leuven, population figures dropped from 300 to 180. In that same period, only five homes were built or renovated there. In Antwerp, the population figure dropped from 300 to 170 between 1671 and 1777. In the 1780s, it appeared that a large increase in population in beguinages was taking place, but this is deceptive since it represented the rehousing of nuns who had formerly been members of congregations and orders abolished by emperor Joseph II (1741-1790). This was followed by the French Revolution, during which time beguinages were abolished because they were not formal religious communities and to enable the selling of their possessions. The government trusted the possessions to the *Commissie van Godshuisen* [Commission for Religious Houses]. Beguines could stay and live there as tenants, but without their distinctive clothing, vows, statutes and without new novices.[92] In some cases, as in Hasselt, the beguines' possessions were sold in public and bought by their generous protectors. The Concordat of Napoleon in 1810 said that beguinage churches

92. Trooskens, 'De begijnenbeweging', p. 45.

that were not yet sold had to be used publicly for parochial services.[93]

From 8 September 1814, beguines were allowed to wear their habits again. They tried to regain ownership of their former possessions but to no avail. Between 1844 and 1862 a political debate between Catholics and Liberals on the issue took place, but this was inconclusive. From then on, the beguine movement began to decline seriously. In 1826 we know of 1879 beguines living in 26 beguinages. In 1896 there were 1308 beguines in fifteen beguinages and by 1978 only fifty beguines in about five courts. Today five elderly beguines remain, all in old people's homes.[94]

| 6 | The Present and Future of the Beguinages (Begijnhoven)

Beguinages are now used for different purposes. The houses themselves are in most cases the property of the OCMW [the municipal departments of social services] which – in the case of Lier, Mechelen and Gent – rents them out to private individuals, mostly to young or poor families. In Aarschot, they have been

---

93. D'HAENENS, *Begijnhoven van België*, p. 7.
94. On the decline: VAN AERSCHOT & HEIRMAN, *Flemish Beguinages*, pp. 42-43 and the short revival in the nineteenth century: *Ibid.*, pp. 50-52.

turned into a museum and an old people's home.[95] In Hasselt, the former beguinage now contains the library and other public services.[96] The Catholic University of Leuven acquired the city's principal beguinage, and turned it into a residence for students, lecturers and visiting lecturers.

Only very recently have the Flemish beguinages become known all over the world, when they became listed among UNESCO's World Heritage Sites. The requisite paperwork was presented by the Flemish Government to UNESCO and subsequently approved in Kyoto, Japan, on 2 December 1989. Because one beguinage cannot be considered as representative of the whole country, thirteen beguinages have been nominated, namely Bruges, Dendermonde, Diest, Hoogstraten, Kortrijk, Lier, Sint-Amandsberg, Sint-Truiden, Tongeren, Turnhout, the *Groot Begijnhof* at Leuven and the *Groot Begijnhof* at Kortrijk and, lastly, the *Klein Begijnhof* at Gent.[97]

95. On Aarschot: *Het begijnhof van Aarschot*, Bijdragen tot de geschiedenis van het Land van Aarschot, 1 (Tielt, 1976); A. PAESSENS, *Aarschot: het Begijnhof* (Aarschot, 1952).

96. On Hasselt : P. DANIELS, 'Notes sur le premier béguinage de Hasselt', *Verzamelde Opstellen* 14 (1937) 25-30; J. LAMBRECHT, *Het oude begijnhof of beknopte geschiedenis van het begijnhof van Hasselt* (Hasselt, 1886).

97. J. GIJSEN, *Vlaamse begijnhoven ontdekken en beleven: Een sfeervolle zoektocht naar een heel eigen verleden* (Aartselaar, 1999), p. 26.

The question is, will the movement be revived again? In 1996 Kathleen Meyers took solemn vows as a beguine in Tienen, aged thirty-one. A priest established a set of special rules for her, consisting of saying the rosary, confession, prayer and humble manual labour. She works with the elderly and those with mental disabilities. This young beguine still lives with her mother, busy with a vocation last seen in Flanders over fifty years ago. But it recalls the origins of the movement eight centuries ago.[98]

---

98. *Ibid.*, p. 25. A weird variant of contemporary Beguines, can be found on the web: the American Beguine Community (http://www.beguine.org/).

| II |
THE SPIRITUALITY
AND MYSTICISM OF THE BEGUINES

| 1 | Introductory Remarks

It is interesting that, already in thirteenth century documents, male clerics talk favourably of the spiritual conversion seemingly typical of women. The thirteenth-century Franciscan friar Lamprecht of Regensburg wrote in his best-known poetical work *Die Tochter von Sion* [*Sion's Daughter* (1238): 'In our days, the *ars* arose in women in Bavaria and Brabant. Lord, what sort of thing can this *ars* be which causes an old woman to understand things more clearly than a cleric possibly could'? Lamprecht expected the cause of this skill or art (*ars*) of the spiritual to lie in the nature of a woman's personality. He also wrote: 'Because of her uncomplicated understanding, her tender heart and her weaker mind, she is more easily fired with enthusiasm, and this in such a way as to make her more able than men to understand the wisdom that comes from heaven'.[1]

1. Quoted in EPINEY-BURGARD & ZUM BRUNN, *Femmes troubadours de Dieu*, p. 6.

Female spirituality of that period was striking. Their mystical experiences focused on love and they expressed their relationship to God using the picture of a wedding metaphorically. Hildegard of Bingen (1098-1179) wrote: 'God cannot be perceived directly, as He is recognised through creation and only by human beings who mirror God's miracles'.[2] Such mystics were once again sensitive to corporality, to nature and to sexuality. Comparing the vocabulary of Hildegard of Bingen, Mechthild of Magdeburg, Hadewijch, Marguerite Porete, Beatrice of Nazareth and others[3] with the notions of courtly love we see clear links. This leads us to recognise that sensuality was an important element of female spirituality of the period.[4] A direct link might be postulated through the influence of *Minne* on several beguine authors. Hadewijch talked about ecstatic experiences during which personal union between the human soul and

2. Quoted in *Ibid.*, p. 104.
3. Beatrice of Nazareth (1200-1268) was raised by beguines but joined the Cistercians. Recently a new edition of her book appeared: R. FAESEN (ed.), *Seven manieren van minne: Middelnederlandse tekst met een inleiding en her-taling* (Kapellen, 1999). Also: *Beatrice of Nazareth and the Thirteenth Century 'Mulieres Religiosae' of the Low Countries*, vol. 1 (Kalamazoo, 1991).
4. The symbolism of courtly love melts into the metaphysical expression of union with God. The culture of the beguines was both religious and secular. Hadewijch in particular masters a courtly use of words (EPINEY-BURGARD & ZUM BRUNN, *Femmes troubadours*, pp. 15 and 20).

God was attained. Her imagery is borrowed from the *Minne*, the central notion of the courtly love lyrics that *Minnesänger* popularised in the German-speaking lands.[5] Hadewijch openly admitted that the desire of God furiously devoured both body and senses. She employed the word *ghevoelen*, which means feeling, experiencing, sensing. This is how she described this experience in her seventh vision:

> Daerna quam hi selve te mi ende nam mi altemale in sine arme ende dwanc mi ane heme. Ende al die lede die ic hadde ghevoelden der siere in al hare ghenoeghen na miere herten begherte ne miere menscheit.[6]
>
> [After that, he came himself to me, took me entirely in his arms, and pressed me to him; and all my members felt his in full felicity, in accordance with the desire of my heart and my humanity.[7]]

Mystical love must always be interpreted as a *vis unitiva* [unifying force]. It was the mystic's response to divine love which dominated this language of love. The language of love was extended, and Mechthild of Magdeburg used expressions such as 'the soul is a mature spouse, that will cast herself naked into God's open arms to be totally embraced and be taken in the nakedness of his limbs'. Mechthild called God

---

5. DE LA CROIX, *L'érotisme au Moyen Âge*, pp. 106-107.
6. Quoted in HADEWIJCH, *Visioenen*, ed. I. DROS & F. WILLAERT (Amsterdam, 1996), p. 82.
7. HART, *Hadewijch*, p. 281.

'my pillow, my love bed, the desire of my glory'.[8] It goes without saying that the Church hierarchy was uneasy with such language. Further, mysticism errs towards quietism, a tendency in Christian mysticism and perfection seeking personal union with the divine by following an inner way to divine union, based on passivity and devotion. The emphasis was on inner prayer and contemplation only, instead of on good works. Even worse, it was thought that works, even good ones, could disturb one's peace of mind. The Church opposed such quietism. It argued that patiently experiencing the mystical union required being both active and passive.

Marguerite Porete, a beguine from Hainaut, was punished with death after her accounts of having direct, unmediated [*sine medio*] contact with God. On 1 July 1310, order from the Inquisition of Paris, she would go to the stake having been convicted by the Bishop of Chambray. Her treatise, the *Miroir des âmes simples et anéanties* [*The Mirror of Simple Souls who are Annihilated*] employed imagery of worldly love to the divine and was, arguably, the most mystical erotic writing of the Middle Ages. By explicitly using *fin amor* as a source of inspiration, she extolled ecstatic love. This way, she became part of a tradition that reacted against the increasing rationalism in scholas-

---

8.   Quoted in P. DINZELBACHER, 'Épouse', DINZELBACHER (ed.), *Dictionnaire de la mystique*, p. 267.

tic theology.[9] In 1312 the Council of Vienne issued the decree *Cum de quibusdam mulieribus* and censured women commonly known as beguines who, as if insane, discoursed on the Trinity and divine essence, leading simple people in error under the pretext of sanctity.[10] With their *subtilitates* and *novitates* they trod on educated theologians' grounds. The latter often saw those mystical works as tracts against the Church. They claimed that beguines suggested that human beings could become perfect on their own, eliminating the mediation of the Church. Mechthild said that people warned her against writing her book *Das fliessende Licht der Gottheit* [The Flowing Light of the Godhead], specifically warning that 'if it is not locked up safely, a fire might rage about it'.[11] She entered a convent just in time for safety reasons. She was well aware that the beguines' autonomous religiosity could eventually endanger them.

The beguines in the Low Countries did not denounce Church practices and never disturbed the peace, though they were sometimes been accused of doing so.[12] Covert quietism is not the only thing

---

9. DE LA CROIX, *L'érotisme au Moyen Âge*, p. 109.
10. Quoted in VAUCHEZ, *La spiritualité*, p. 167.
11. HADEWIJCH, *Visioenen*, p. 13.
12. J. WEISMAYER, 'Quiétisme', DINZELBACHER (ed.), *Dictionnaire de la mystique*, p. 665.

that was held against them. Beguine mystical language was very easy to misinterpret and many different religious people were hostile towards the beguine movement. Hadewijch had to fight three forms of criticism: firstly, the *mulieres religiosae* claimed that God's presence was physically perceivable. Hadewijch wrote in her 'seventh vision' that 'her limbs were trembling and shaking with desire'. This direct access to God threatened the mediatory role of the clergy. Secondly, many clerics had difficulties understanding the jubilation, the mystical ecstasy which is frequently described. Thirdly, the independence of beguines challenged contemporary social norms. Beguines recruited wealthy women who would rather abandon all wealth and enter a court than marry. Some women even divorced their spouse or patiently waited till they were widowed. Eventually, they were forced to conform to one of the three socially endorsed alternatives: submission to obeying priests, marriage, or enclosure in religious orders.[13]

Beguines wrote in the vernacular. This too was problematic and generally disapproved of by the Church authorities as it challenged the clergy's teaching and preaching function. Of course, their works circulated widely, and were considered to be theo-

13. MOMMAERS, *Hadewijch*, pp. 40-55.

logically well-founded.[14] The influential canonry of St. Victor in Paris recognised that these mystical writings were innovative. Victorine scholars adapted the works and by using allegorical methods of explanation, they reconciled the rational logic of traditional theology with mysticism.[15]

| 2 | The Earliest Beguine Writers

Beguine spirituality was by no means solely mystical. Contrary to what is often claimed, most beguines were acquainted with theology and metaphysics. They attempted to combine religious doctrine with religious experience.[16] Few beguines were mystical writers, but until the eighteenth century the phe-

14. In the Low Countries vernacular Bibles first appeared in the thirteenth century. See T. COUN, 'De Zuidnederlandse vertaling van de vier evangeliën', T. MERTENS (ed.), *Boeken voor de eeuwigheid: Middelnederlands geestelijk proza*, Nederlandse literatuur en cultuur in de Middeleeuwen, 8 (Amsterdam, 1993), pp. 87-107.
15. This was a period of real tension between theology on one hand and philosophy and mysticism on the other. On the school of Saint Victor in Paris: F. BONNARD, *Histoire de l'Abbaye royale et de l'ordre des chanoines réguliers de Saint Victor de Paris*, 2 vol. (Paris, 1904-1907) and J. LONGÈRE, *L'abbaye parisienne de Saint-Victor au moyen âge*, Bibliotheca Victorina, 1 (Paris, 1991).
16. EPINEY-BURGARD & ZUM BRUNN, *Femmes troubadours*, pp. 6 and 9.

nomenon would remain linked with the beguine movement. Short biographies of Mechthild of Magdeburg, Beatrice of Nazareth and Geertrui of Oosten emphasise this feature of their spirituality, whilst Hadewijch was widely renown.

Mechthild of Magdeburg (ca. 1208-1282/97) was of distinguished descent and came from the German diocese of Magdeburg. At a young age she left home to devote and dedicate her life to God. For thirty years, she remained silent about the mystical mercy she had been receiving since the age of twelve. Then in 1215 her Dominican confessor forced her to write everything down. These writings caused her to have enemies as well as admirers. In 1270 she entered the Cistercian convent at Helfta, where she met amongst others the mystic Gertrude of Helfta (1256-1301/02). In Mechthild's mysticism we can see the love of God made explicit but familial: 'her father by nature, her brother by his human nature and her bridegroom because of love'. She explored new imagery in *Das fliessende Licht der Gottheit* to describe a God who burns with desire and draws her soul to him in a union that is so strong it makes the human soul stop realising it is still on earth.[17]

17. V. ZÜHLSDORFF, 'Mechthilde de Magdebourg', DINZELBACHER (ed.), *Dictionnaire de la mystique*, pp. 525-527.

Beatrice of Nazareth (ca. 1200-1268), who was beatified, came from a wealthy, patrician family from Tienen.[18] After her mother's death she was raised by beguines and later by Cistercians in the village of Florival, where she took her solemn vows in 1216. In 1221 she withdrew in isolation in Maagdendal, a convent in Tienen, and in 1236 she moved to Nazareth, a new nunnery in Lier, where she became prioress. In her autobiography she described her internal life characterised by extreme asceticism, *imitatio Christi*, devotion to the Eucharist and ecstatic phenomena. The original work is now lost, but quotations are still found in other books. What we do have by her is a complete but small tract *Van seven manieren van minnen [On Seven Ways of Loving]*. Together with Hadewijch's *Visioenen [Visions]*, these are the oldest Middle Dutch texts that have been preserved.[19]

18. On some aspects of the disappeared beguinage of Tienen: P. DEWAHLENS, 'Folklore et légendes de Tienen', *Folklore Brabançon* 31 (1959) 106-131 and MOULAERT, 'Règle et statuts du béguinage de Tirlemont aux 16e et 17e siècles', *Analectes pour servir à l'histoire ecclésiastique de la Belgique* 6 (1870) 142-175 ; C. VAN BASTEN BATENBURG, *Registrum Mortuorum Ecclesiae Begginasii Oppidi Thenensis*, Tablettes du Brabant, 1 (Hombeek, 1956), pp. 171-191.

19. F. WILLAERT, 'Béatrice de Nazareth', DINZELBACHER (ed.), *Dictionnaire de la mystique*, pp. 93-94.

One of the best known mystic beguines of the fourteenth century is the beatified Gertrude of Oosten (ca. 1300-1358) from Delft. In 1340 she received stigmata during an intense periode of devotion to the Passion of Christ. On her request the stigmata disappeared. She had the gift of prophecy.[20] She wrote forty-five meditations as well as a number of hymns, which unfortunately are now lost. We know almost nothing of her life.

There were also occasional impostors. In the diocese of Metz, Sibilla Beguina of Marsal pretended to be a holy beguine who stayed alive without eating and who had visions of Michael the Archangel. A Dominican monk discovered the deception and she was convicted. She was walled in for life and put on bread and water. She died shortly after her conviction.[21]

| 3 | Early Beguine Spirituality and Devotion to the Person of Jesus

In the early Middle Ages the image of God was strongly inspired by the Old Testament image of a militant, judgemental Yahweh. In the late twelfth century the interest moved to the suffering God in Jesus the man. In iconography the glorified Christ triumphant on the cross was replaced by scenes depicting

20. P. DINZELBACHER, 'Gertrude d'Oosten', DINZELBACHER (ed.), *Dictionnaire de la mystique*, p. 332.
21. L. J. M. PHILIPPEN, 'Begijnhoven en spiritualiteit', 177-179.

the horror of his crucifixion. The body of Christ was portrayed in distorted, tormented poses to emphasise the humanity he shared with us. Mary of Oignies (the first recognisable beguine) and Odilia of Liège held this view of Jesus.[22]

The affective experiencing of Jesus's birth dates back to the same period. In 1223 St. Francis introduced a crib in the church. This Christocentrism which emphasised Christ's devotion to humankind became among the mystics an individual and intimate experience of God.[23] The works by Ida of Leuven (d.

---

22. Marie of Oignies is not an exception, see M. H. KING, 'The Desert Mothers Revisited', *Vox Benedictina* 5 (1988) 325-354 and J. DOR et al., *New Trends in Feminine Spirituality. The Holy Women of Liège and Their Impact*, (Turnhout, 1999). In the thirteenth century, a new hagiographical genre comes into being: the *vitae* of holy women. No longer martyrs of the first centuries of Christianity, nor royal figures, but biographies of female representatives of the *vita apostolica*, all known by their hagiographers. In the 'Belgian' region, thirteen of those biographies are known: Mary of Oignies (the first with such a hagiography), Lutgardis of Aywières or Tongeren, Christine of St. Truiden, Margareth of Ieper, Beatrice of Nazareth, Ida of Nivelles, Ida of Léau (=Zoutleeuw), Ida of Leuven, Alice of Schaarbeek, Julian of Cornillon, Juette of Huy, Elisabeth of Spalbeek, and Catherine of Leuven. See also A.VAUCHEZ, *La sainteté en Occident aux derniers siècles du Moyen Âge d'après les procès de canonisation et les documents hagiographiques* (Paris, 1981).
23. JANSSENS & MATHEEUWSEN, *Renaissance in veelvoud*, pp. 162-165.

ca. 1300) showed a clear interest in the Infant Jesus.
Many others proclaimed themselves as the foster
mother of Jesus.[24] The interest in Jesus as a human
being could not be separated from the *vita apostolica*.
As explained above, these beguines pursued a new
sort of spiritual life and voluntary poverty and disliked outward trappings and pageantry. They
preferred to do manual labour and works of mercy
and their apostolic dedication ensured they focused
directly on Jesus Christ.[25]

Ecstatic mysticism is typical of the first beguines.
But mysticism was not their only spiritual practice.
Earlier on, we mentioned that the beguines' devotion
for Christ led to a popular new cult of the Eucharist.
Around Liège, where this eucharistic piety was con-

24. On that spirituality: M. LAUWERS, 'Paroles de femmes, sain-
    teté féminine. L'église du 13ᵉ siècle face aux béguines', G.
    BRAIVE & J.-M. CAUCHIES (eds.), *La critique historique à
    l'épreuve: Liber discipulorum Jacques Paquet* (Brussels,
    1989), pp. 99-115.
25. VAN MIERLO, 'Losse beschouwingen', p. 129. In the art of
    beguines and nuns of that period, Christocentrism became
    dominant, with a special emphasis on his suffering as a
    human being. It has even been argued that the figure of
    the Pietà – the suffering Mother Mary with the dead Christ
    on her knees – came into being in beguine circles (P. VAN-
    DENBROECK, *Hooglied: De beeldwereld van religieuze
    vrouwen in de Zuidelijke Nederlanden, vanaf de 13ᵈᵉ eeuw*
    [Gent, 1994], p. 32 and J. E. ZIEGLER, *Sculpture of
    Compassion: The Pieta and the Beguines in the Southern
    Low Countries c. 1300-c. 1600* [Brussels, 1992]).

centrated, many recluses let themselves be walled in against the church walls. At this period the practice of holding the host in the tabernacle and heightened liturgical emphasis on the elevation of the host increased the desire in ordinary people to see the host.[26] Following the recluses example, the beguines too showed more interest in the eucharist. The renewed devotion to the Eucharist led to practices that were very unusual for that period, for exemple weekly communion.[27] Another parallel with recluses was the devotion to the Holy Trinity.[28]

| 4 | Hadewijch of Antwerp

Dilectus meus mihi et ego illi /
Ego dilecto meo et dilectus meus mihi
[Song of Songs 2:16 and 6:2].[29]

Hadewijch has been called 'one of the most gifted and intellectually inclined mystical poets of the thirteenth

---

26. AXTERS, *Geschiedenis van de vroomheid*, part 1, pp. 302-303.
27. *Ibid.*, pp. 321-322.
28. *Ibid.*, p. 302.
29. 'My beloved is mine and I am his / I am my beloved's and my beloved is mine'. These are the central lines of Scripture that occur most frequently in Hadewijch's works (M. VAN BAEST, *Poetry of Hadewijch*, Studies in Spirituality: Supplement, 3 [Leuven, 1998], p. 26).

century',[30] but as hardly any contemporary, independent documents have been preserved, very little is known about this outstanding literary figure.[31] This limits us to what she writes about herself in her extant works: forty-five stanzaic poems, or *Strofische Gedichten* [*Strophic Poems*], sixteen *Mengeldichten*

30. J. R. STRAYER, *Dictionary of the Middle Ages* (New York, 1982), p. 44. It is not clear whether she really was a beguine. Recent research revealed that she might have been a Cistercian sister (R. FAESEN, *Lichaam in lichaam, ziel in ziel: Christusbeleving bij Hadewijch en haar tijdgenoten* Baarn and Gent, 2003, pp. 14-23). Even if she was not a beguine, the beguines were strongly influenced by her spirituality.

31. Some English monographs on Hadewijch: J. G. MILHAVEN, *Hadewijch and her Sisters: Other Ways of Loving and Knowing* (New York, 1993); B. MCGINN (ed.), *Meister Eckhart and the Beguine Mystics: Hadewijch of Brabant, Mechthild of Magdeburg, and Marguerite Porete* (New York, 1994); T. M. GUEST, *Some Aspects of Hadewijch's Poetic Form in the 'Strofische gedichten'*, Bibliotheca neerlandica extra muros, 3 (The Hague, 1975) and S. M. MURK JANSEN, *The Measure of Mystic Thought: A Study of Hadewijch's Mengeldichten*, Göppinger Arbeiten zur Germanistik, 536 (Göppingen, 1991). P. MOMMAERS, *Hadewijch: Writer, Beguine, Love Mystic* (Leuven, 2004). For editions and translations one can consult in English an edition of the stanzaic poems by M. VAN BAEST, *Poetry of Hadewijch*; HART, *Hadewijch*; F. BOWIE (ed.), *Beguine Spirituality: Mystical Writings of Mechthild of Magdeburg, Beatrice of Nazareth, and Hadewijch of Brabant* (New York, 1990); and J. HIRSHFIELD (ed.), *Women in Praise of the Sacred* (Dewey, 1994).

[*Mixed Poems*], thirty-one prose *Brieven* [*Letters*] and principally her prose work entitled *Visioenen* [*Visions*] comprising fourteen mystical visions. The *Letters* and *Visions* often mention details of her personal experiences. From the type of advice she gives in her letters, we can also sense her personality.

The so-called *Mixed Poems* are in fact poetic letters in rhymed couplets. Many of these letters do not have an addressee, so we could consider them as small tracts. In medieval literature, it is often difficult to draw the boundary between spiritual letters and pious tracts. It is also clear that her letters were meant for friends of the same faith with whom she had a good relationship. The terms of address give evidence of openness: *suete* or *lieve minne* [sweet or dear love], *hertelike lieve* [heart-felt love], *lieve herte* [beloved heart/friend] or *lieve kint* [beloved child]. In her letters, Hadewijch portrays herself as a kind friend, a wise guide and above all as God's passionate mistress.[32] At the same time, her literary work, even the hyper-stylised stanzaic poems, were means to unite groups of beguines.[33]

For some time the *Stanzaic Poems*, a corpus of divine poetry, has been considered to be an individual expression of her deepest emotions, although this reflects romantic scholarship of the nineteenth or early twentieth century. The poems were meant as

32. HADEWIJCH, *Visioenen*, p. 15.
33. F. VAN OOSTROM, *Aanvaard dit werk: Over Middelnederlandse auteurs en hun publiek*, Nederlandse literatuur en cultuur in de middeleeuwen, 6 (Amsterdam, 1992), p. 23.

instructions or guidelines to her readers, because the complaining, mourning or longing 'I' person always does exactly what Hadewijch called the only correct way of loving.[34]

Hadewijch's *Visions* are not open to simple biographical interpretation. Mystical women had certain experiences that aroused suspicion among outsiders. For example a loss of sense of expression, telepathy, levitation, glossolalia, clairvoyance, visions and other unusual psychosomatic experiences.[35] These are incidental side-products of a true mystical life.[36] Hadewijch's visions are described within meticulously composed texts far removed from the immediate experience. The *Visions* attempt to describe her ascendance in love and her growth in mystical maturity.[37]

Hadewijch's book of *Visions* does offer some information about her life and times within the appendix to the work, the 'List of Perfects', which is a list of people who experienced *minne* [love in the particular meaning we will describe later] in a perfect way. This list contains names of people who lived shortly before

34. HADEWIJCH, *Visioenen*, pp. 16-17.
35. When Hadewijch envisions God as Lady Minne, then the role of Lady Minne is far from the passive, powerless, and submissive one thought to be proper for a woman in those days. God is presented as a Lady and that Lady is neither submissive, nor powerless. VAN BAEST, *Poetry of Hadewijch*, p. 15.
36. *Ibid.*, p. 3.
37. HADEWIJCH, *Visioenen*, pp. 17-18.

Hadewijch, and who died somewhat earlier than her or were her contemporaries. It offers a dating for the work, because *meester Robbaert* [Master Robert] who had a beguine killed for experiencing true *minne* is mentioned in these writings. This *Robbaert* is Robert le Bougre, leader of the Inquisition in Flanders between 1235 and 1238. Further down the list, Hadewijch mentions some anchorites who were living next to the city walls of Jerusalem; but in 1244 Jerusalem fell into Saracen hands. We may safely conclude that Hadewijch had drawn up the list before 1244, and after 1238. The Book of *Visions* also localises the work. It states that Hadewijch sent Lord Henry of Breda to the anchoress Mina. The lords of Breda lived in Antwerp during the thirteenth century. Moreover, the work is written in a Brabantine dialect.

More biographical information may be gleaned. She must have belonged to a prosperous class because she speaks her *Diets* (Middle Dutch) mother-tongue perfectly. She even interprets Latin texts and is familiar with all aspects of the French *chansons d'amour*. In the *Stanzaic Poems*, for example, she expresses the mutuality of the partnership as a human being with God in the social context of chivalry and its codes.[38] Her writings show her

---

38. VAN BAEST, *Poetry of Hadewijch*, p. 15. We have mentioned already that her language can be very erotic; Milhaven speaks of 'bodily knowing' (MILHAVEN, *Hadewijch and her Sisters, passim*).

familiarity with noble terminology and have an aristocratic attitude. Maybe Hadewijch belonged to the nobility, but if she did not, she was at least part of the patrician class of some city in Brabant.[39]

We can also determine from her writings that she was a beguine and a mistress of a beguine group. Twice in the *Visions*, Hadewijch describes herself with characteristics of a *mulier religiosa* in the technical meaning of the word. At the beginning of the first vision, we can read:[40]

> Het was in enen sondage ter octaven van Pentecosten dat men mi Onsen Here heimelike te minen bedde brachte, omdat ic ghevoelde soe grote treckinghe van binnen van minen gheeste, dat ic mi van buten onder de menschen soe vele niet gehebben en conste dat icker ghegaen ware.
>
> [It was a Sunday, in the Octave of Pentecost, when our Lord was brought secretly to my bedside, because I felt such an attraction of my spirit inwardly that I could not control myself outwardly in a degree sufficient to go among persons; it would have been impossible for me to go among them.]

And the first sentence of the Seventh Vision says:[41]

> Te enen cinxendaghe wart mi vertoent in de dagheraet. Ende men sanc mettunen in de kerke ende ic was daer.

---

39. MOMMAERS, *Hadewijch*, pp. 18-21.
40. Quoted in HADEWIJCH, *Visioenen*, p. 32. Translation: HART, *Hadewijch*, p. 263.
41. Quoted in HADEWIJCH, *Visioenen*, p. 78. Translation: HART, *Hadewijch*, p. 280.

[On a certain Pentecost Sunday I had a vision at dawn. Matins were being sung in the church, and I was present.]

This means that Hadewijch lived in the vicinity of a church where the office was sung and this can only be a conventual or a collegiate church. It was probably the latter because she had to go among people to receive the host. Eventually, she received communion brought to her bed as she became too ill to get up. The church she mentioned can hardly be a conventual church because she would not be mixing with laity and she was certainly not a nun. She seemed to be living in a small community of beguines and maybe she herself had founded such a community in Antwerp. In Letter 5, she wrote:[42]

> Ay, dat en si u geen wonder, al eest mi wee, dattie gene, die wi vercoren hebben met ons in jubileerne in onse Lief, dat si ons hier beginnen te stoorne ende te brekene onse geselscap omme gescheden te sine, ende nameleec mi deese met niemand en willen laten.
>
> [Oh, do not be surprised if it pains me that those we had chosen to rejoice with us in our Beloved are beginning to interfere with us here and to destroy our company in order to disband us, and especially me, whom they wish to leave with no one!]

---

42. Quoted in HADEWIJCH, *Een bloemlezing uit haar werken*, ed. N. DE PAEPE (Amsterdam and Brussels, 1979), p. 67. Translation: HART, *Hadewijch*, pp. 55-56.

Hadewijch seems to have belonged to the *beghinae disciplinatae,* the enclosed beguines who lived
together in small houses scattered across the town.[43]
A phrase in Letter 25 could prove this:[44]

> Segget Margrieten (...) datse hare trecke ter volmaac-
> theit waart ende gereide hare met ons te wonenne daar
> wi versamenen selen, ende datse metten vreemden niet
> en wone noch en blive.
> [Tell Margriet (...) that she apply herself to the attain-
> ment of perfection and prepare herself to live with us,
> where we shall one day be together; and she should nei-
> ther live nor remain with aliens.]

We can gather from Hadewijch's writings that she
was a guide in *minne* to other people. This can be
deduced from the fact that she often had to defend
her group against discontent outsiders, but also
against other members. Letter 23 is addressed to
somebody who left a community in turmoil to live in
another community. In this Letter, Hadewijch mentions that some beguines dislike her and want to
dismiss her, apparently in jealousy against the intense
loyalty which she inspired among some fellows. In
Hadewijch's works reasons for these quarrels can
be traced. The matter at issue was authentic experience of God, the *gherechte minne.* Not everybody
agreed with Hadewijch's approach and some wanted
to push through their own ways of dealing with

43. MOMMAERS, *Hadewijch,* pp. 21-22.
44. Quoted in HADEWIJCH, *Een bloemlezing uit haar werken,*
    p. 126. Translation: HART, *Hadewijch,* p. 106.

minne. The bones of contention focused on the spiritual journey that led to self-satisfaction, on the balance between passivity and the active expression of love, and on particular practices.

The first problem Hadewijch deals with is how religious *genoechte* [satisfaction] is revealed. At the start of Letter 23 the problem is outlined and the author gives her friends the following advice:[45]

> Also enich levet der heileger Minnen om pure Minne, niet om uw genoechte siere Minnen te plegene in uwer oefeningen, mer in die werken sijns te plegene die Minnen genoegen.
>
> [Live thus exclusively for holy Love out of pure love, not because of the satisfaction you might find by communing with his love in your devout exercises, but in order to devote yourself to God himself in the works that content Love.]

The experiencing of *minne* cannot be about one's own satisfaction, but has to be about satisfying God. If not, it will only lead to self-satisfaction. Then, experience can never transcend itself. Someone who seeks satisfaction through *minne* has to give herself to the Beloved One by doing all sorts of work. Experience for sake of the experience has to be prevented. Letter 24 contains a warning:[46]

> Ic sal u seggen sonder voegen: en laat u niet men dan Minne genoegen. (...) Ende en versuumt u aan gene

45. HADEWIJCH, *Een bloemlezing uit haar werken*, p. 121. Translation: HART, *Hadewijch*, p. 102.
46. HADEWIJCH, *Een bloemlezing uit haar werken*, p. 122. Translation: HART, *Hadewijch*, p. 103.

genoechte, daarbi u redene te verliesene; uwe redene
die ic meine dat es, dat gi uwe kennesse altoos wakende
selt houden in onderscheidicheiden.
[I will tell you without beating about the bush: Be satisfied with nothing less than Love. Give reason its time,
and always observe where you heed it too little and
where enough.]

Letter 10 also warns against the danger of mistak-
ing lust for mystical love. Ten years later, Mechthild
of Magdeburg started to write for her own group of
followers mainly for the same reason. She is angry
about a particular beguine who thinks she does not
need human advice anymore. Selfish feelings prevent
true encounters with God. They obstruct the lover's
view and block the way towards *minne*.[47] It is nothing more than self-centredness under the pretext of
spirituality. In Mechthild's opinion, true love for God
is persistent and totally faithful, but the only possible reward is *minne* itself.[48]

The second problem results from the first. People
who want to experience God's grace without crav-
ing for it can suffer from two ailments that make them
inhuman. They can either be totally engrossed in
experience, so that they will become passive, or they
can plunge into activist action, so they cannot leave
anyone alone. Several times, Hadewijch warns

47. VAN BAEST, *Poetry of Hadewijch*, pp. 25-26.
48. M. E. WAITHE, *A History of Women Philosophers: Medieval,
Renaissance and Enlightenment, AD 500-1600* (Amsterdam,
1989), p. 145.

against either side.[49] Three examples are from Letter 23, Letter 15 and Letter 24:[50]

Sijt vroed nu daar gi sijt; gi hebbes wel te doene. Ende boven alle dinc bevelic u dat gi u hoedet daar herde wiseleke van sonderlingheiden, diere daar herde vele es.

[Behave yourself wisely where you now are; this is certainly needful for you. Above all things I counsel you to withhold yourself very prudently from eccentricities, which are very numerous there.]

... so en sijt nummer so coene dat gi u enich sonderlinges wesens onderwindet sonder raat van geesteleken vroeden.
[... never be so reckless as to undertake anything exceptional without counsel from persons of spiritual wisdom.]

Ic sal u seggen sonder voegen: en laat u niet men dan Minne genoegen.
[I will tell you without beating about the bush: Be satisfied with nothing less than Love.]

Hadewijch reacts against exaggerated passivity and gushing altruism in scathing terms. Indeed, one can err in love and charity. Letter 4 is plain:[51]

In caritaten doolt men in onbeschedenen dienste van gevene bi onsten sonder noot, van dienen sonder noot; ende dat een mensche hem selven quetset sonder noot. Vele doet affectie datmen caritate noemt.

49. MOMMAERS, *Hadewijch*, pp. 59-65.
50. Quoted in HADEWIJCH, *Een bloemlezing uit haar werken*, pp. 95 and 121-122. Translation: HART, *Hadewijch*, pp. 79 and 103.
51. Quoted in HADEWIJCH, *Een bloemlezing uit haar werken*, p. 65. Translation: HART, *Hadewijch*, p. 54.

[In charity men err through injudicious service, for instance when they give out of mere liking where there is no need, or render superfluous service, or weary themselves when there is no need. Often emotional attraction motivates what is called charity.]

Hadewijch's main activity was guiding her community. Writing was a duty and responsibility that she bore as part of her pastoral care.[52] Hadewijch was not a lonely mystic, as Van Mierlo argued, happy in complete union with God, totally transcendent, proclaiming her service to *minne* in some hyper-personal love lyric intended for posterity. Frank Willaert has emphasised that Hadewijch wrote in a particular context. Her poetry had a specific function and concentrated on the spiritual development of her friends and the poetry was meant for that setting.[53] Nonetheless, this practical function notwithstanding her writing demonstrates literary quality.[54]

Hadewijch was soon recognised as a great mystic author.[55] During the Middle Ages her work was well-

---

52. F. Van Oostrom, *Aanvaard dit werk* (Amsterdam, 1992), p. 71.
53. *Ibid.*, pp. 122-124.
54. J. B. Oosterman, *De gratie van het gebed: Overlevering en functie van Middelnederlandse berijmde gebeden*, Nederlandse literatuur en cultuur in de middeleeuwen, 12 (Amsterdam, 1995), p. 147.
55. Middle-Dutch spiritual prose started with mystic prose from Hadewijch and Beatrice of Nazareth. T. Mertens (ed.), *Boeken voor de eeuwigheid: Middelnederlands geestelijk proza*, Nederlandse literatuur en cultuur in de middeleeuwen, 8 (Amsterdam, 1993), p. 20.

9. Leuven. In the seventeenth century, many churches
and interiors have been restored in the popular baroque style

10. Diest. Interior of St. Catherine's.
Stucco and altar (s. XVIII)

11. Turnhout. Reconstruction of a beguine kitchen
in the Museum of the beguinage (s. XVII-XX)

12. Leuven. Water is an important element
for each beguinage

13. Sint-Truiden. Church of St. Agnes
with XIII-XVII c. frescoes

14. Leuven. Taking the vows (s. XVII)
(K.U.Leuven, Kunstpatrimonium, collection 'Groot Begijnhof')
(photo Paul Laes, Rotselaar)

15. Auguste Oleffe (1865-1931), Beguinage of Nieuwpoort, now disappeared *(private collection)*

16. Carolus Tremerie, Mortuary of the
Small Beguinage of Gent (1899).
Gent, Museum voor Schone Kunsten
(Copyright IRPA-KIK Brussel)

regarded by the Carthusians, the regular canons and by the circles of the *devotio moderna*. She exercised influence on John of Ruusbroec (1293-1381) and his disciple John of Leeuwen (ca. 1314-1378). At the end of the Middle Ages excerpts of Hadewijch's work circulated under the name of *Sante Adelwip* or *Sant Adel*. But later her writings passed into oblivion. It was not until 1838, when the nineteenth-century Germanic philologist François-Joseph Mone rediscovered a manuscript, that Hadewijch was introduced to the canon of Middle Dutch literature.[56] Together with Ruusbroec, she is one of the most important mystics of the Low Countries.[57] Thanks to the scholar Jozef van Mierlo (1878-1958), every Dutch-speaking secondary-school student is familiar with her poetic talent.

| 5 | Hadewijch's Mysticism

Hadewijch was a mystic. This may suggest something obscure and shady, something sacrosanct, irrational and unearthly. But mystics struggled, to express in words, something that is ineffable, an experience that

---

56. K. WILSON, *Medieval Women Writers* (Manchester, 1984), p. 191.
57. F. WILLAERT, 'Hadewijch', DINZELBACHER (ed.), *Dictionnaire de la mystique*, p. 632.

is beyond words.[58] Somebody like Hadewijch speaks
plainly and never uses confusing terms or images,
with regard to God's mystical experience.[59] Mysticism
is all about a broadened perception. The mystic 'feels',
'smells', 'sees' and 'tastes' God, because he or she has
been touched by the hand of God. So, mysticism is not
a matter of rational cognition, but of the intense experiencing of that cognition, in other words, an
intensified consciousness. Hadewijch experiences
that God lives in her and that she is aware of that in-
dwelling. This qualifies Hadewijch as a mystic. She
possesses everything she already has with her total
psyche and she becomes what she in fact truly is. She
warrants the description of being a mystic because
she is able to devote so many pages to describing the
extreme nearness or the 'in-dwelling' of God.[60] She
has an enormous linguistic power and talent to
express, many emotions and insights in words and
images that never before have been expressed in her
Middle-Dutch mother-tongue.[61]

Hadewijch's root-metaphor in her works is *minne*,
which means 'God is Love'. Other mystics use the
Johannine metaphor of *light,* which Hadewijch also
knows, but she prefers to speak of *minne. De minne
is al* [love is all], she writes at the end of Letter 25.

58. VAN BAEST, *Poetry of Hadewijch*, p. 21.
59. MOMMAERS, *Hadewijch.*, pp. 90-95.
60. *Ibid.*
61. VAN BAEST, *Poetry of Hadewijch*, p. 5.

This word allows diverse meanings, and is so broad that it has several semantic layers at one time. *Minne* is a noun as well as a verb and Hadewijch never hesistates to use simultaneously the different meanings of *minne*. *Minne* is first about the Godhead as such, but God as *minne* is expressed through Jesus and *minne*. *Minne* sometimes appears to be the innermost core of a person. Furthermore, *minne* is used to describe the relationship between God and human beings, or the covenant between God and Hadewijch and so on.[62]

Hadewijch finds different ways to make us understand that her experience was not the result of a particular effort. The experience suddenly encaptured her. This does not mean that preparations are superfluous. Hadewijch always keeps stimulating her followers to practise the virtues and to do good works. *Minne* reveals itself when it pleases to do so, but in anticipation of its coming, people have to serve and to seek it.[63] That includes a certain passivity.

Hadewijch uses the term 'passivity' least of all in the sense of tranquillity. Passivity means an experience that can only be received by submitting to it or leaving the initiative to God. Passivity does not mean that all human activity comes to a stop, but that activity will be overwhelmed by the superabundance when it arrives. Suddenly there will be too much wealth at one

62. *Ibid.*, pp. 5,10, 35-36.
63. MOMMAERS, *Hadewijch*, pp. 96-98.

time. Ordinary people know God via imagery, and so by mediation. Mystics know God immediately and in an unmediated way. For Hadewijch the essence of the Good News is the union of God and human beings. But Hadewijch struggles to express the *enicheit* [union] which she experiences in words, so that her beguines could grow on the spiritual path of mysticism. Despite her own clear language, she regularly warns her followers against the excessive use of words, because what is actually happening inside cannot be framed into language. Thus, it is not surprising that we know of more mystics than of mystical tracts.

The silent enjoyment of the unity with God involves stillness and the mystic only utters words when he/she is forced to do so.[64] One quotation will do (Letter 8):[65]

> Ende hi sal swigen, alse hi gerne sprake; ende alse hi gerne pensde omme gebruken sal hi spreken, ommedat men Minne om minne nit en berespe. Ende hi soude liever wee dogen boven macht dan hem een point gebrake vander minnen ere (...)
> [He shall be silent when he would gladly have spoken, and speak when he would gladly have fixed his thought on divine fruition, in order that no one blame the Beloved on account of his love. He ought rather to suffer woe beyond his strength than to fail on any point relating to the honour of Love.]

64. Mommaers, *Hadewijch*, pp. 90-95.
65. Hadewijch, *Een bloemlezing uit haar werken*, p. 80. Translation: Hart, *Hadewijch*, p. 65.

The stillness of the mystic makes it possible to hear God (Letter 18):[66]

> Ende also doen noch diegene die in vrihede der Minnen dienen; sie rusten op die soete wise borst ende sien ende horen die heimelike woorde die onvertelleec ende onge- hoort sijn dan volke, overmids die soete runings des heilichs Geests.
>
> [And this is what they do who serve Love in liberty; they rest on that sweet, wise breast and see and hear hidden words – which are ineffable and unheard-of by men – through the sweet whisper of the Holy Spirit.]

The experience of hearing God is special. In divine speech, one word is spoken, the Word. In that respect the mystic gains no information or rational truths. Words are not spoken, insights not given. The Word is not spoken, but happens. Something is effectuated. The heard Word is a divine touch [*gherinen*] that is more than psychological agitation. It consists of the essential in-flowing of God into human beings.[67]

The stillness and unpreparedness that precedes the mystical experience was Hadewijch's own expe- rience. At the beginning of the first vision, she writes[68]:

> Daer was ic te kinsche toe ende te ongewassen ende ic hadder niet genoch toe ghepijnt noch gheleeft int ghetal van soe hogher werdecheit alse daertoe behoerde ende

66. *Ibid.*, p. 109. Translation: HART, *Hadewijch*, p. 88.
67. MOMMAERS, *Hadewijch*, pp. 90-95.
68. HADEWIJCH, *Visioenen*, p. 32. Translation: HART, *Hadewijch*, p. 263.

alse mi daer wel vertoent wart doe endi mi noch wel sci-
jnt.

[For this I was still too childish and too little grown-up;
and I had not as yet sufficiently suffered for it or lived
the number of years requisite for such exceptional wor-
thiness. That is what was shown to me then and still
seems the same to me.]

She considers herself to be too young and too imma-
ture. That is not surprising, since she received her
first mystical experiences at the age of ten.[69] During
her search for the *minne*, she received a promise and
a commandment. The promise was that she would
become God's Bride only if she brought her opinions
into conformity with the divine will. The commandment was a positive version of the prohibition:
Hadewijch would only taste the delight of being one
with God, if she started resembling him in his, that
is Christ's, humanity (Letter 28):[70]

Ic sach Gode God ende den mensche mensche. Ende
doen en wonderde mi niet, dat God God was, ende dat
de mensche mensche was. Doen sagic Gode mensche
ende ic sach den mensche godlec. Doen en wonderde
mi niet dattie mensche verweent was met Gode.

69. In Letter 11 she writes: '[ ] from my tenth year onward I
have been caught so closely in heart-felt love that it would
have been the death of me within the first two years after
its beginning, had not God given me a strength more
exceptional than the strength of common folk and had not
he healed my nature again with his being'. Quoted in VAN
BAEST, *Poetry of Hadewijch*, pp. 23-24.
70. HADEWIJCH, *Een bloemlezing uit haar werken*, pp. 136-137.

[I saw God as God and humanity as human. And then I did not wonder that God was God and humanity human. And then I saw God as human and humanity as godlike. And then I did not wonder that humanity was joined to God in radiant glory.][71]

In other words, she had to be prepared to live a life of pain and suffering, like Jesus, who faithfully and until the bitter end followed the will of his Father. The key to the perfect love which unites God and human beings is not the experience of God's presence, as she thought earlier in her inexperience, but the devotion to God's will as Jesus showed us. That explains her never-ending ardour to warn against passivity.[72]

71. Quoted in VAN BAEST, *Poetry of Hadewijch*, p. 31.
72. HADEWIJCH, *Visioenen*, p. 21.

| III |

DAILY LIFE IN THE BEGUINAGE

| 1 | Architecture

Most beguinages had to be rebuilt in the seventeenth century, after their destruction during the religious conflicts of the previous century.[1] However they retained certain medieval features such as their location, structure and the building plan and location of the church. There were three main types of beguine architecture: beguinages with a town pattern, court beguinages and miscellaneous beguinages. The first type contained beguinages that were structured as a town and consisted of smaller roads. (Brussels, Diest, the Great Beguinage of Gent, Ieper, Leuven, Lier, the Small Beguinage of Mechelen and Tongeren.) One parcel remained as cemetery. Beguinages of the second type, court beguinages, had houses that were gathered around a central court,

1. Unless otherwise mentioned, this part is based on M. TROOSKENS, 'Begijnen in de Moderne en Hedendaagse Tijd', M. WYNANTS (ed.), *Begijnen en begijnhoven* (Brussels, 1994), pp. 73-111. An English overview on beguine architecture in all its aspects, see chapter 3 of VAN AERSCHOT & HEIRMAN, *Flemish Beguinages*.

often with trees in it. Such triangular court types can be found in Aalst, Aarschot, Anderlecht, Bruges, Dendermonde, Diksmuide, Hasselt, Herentals, Hoogstraten, Oudenaarde, Sint-Amandsberg and Turnhout. If the houses were built in two parallel rows surrounding a piece of lawn, we are dealing with a miscellaneous type (Antwerp, Kortrijk, Sint-Truiden and Tienen).[2] They lay outside the town ramparts, until after the town's expansion.

Beguinages (*curtes beguinales*) have some typical elements such as a church, an infirmary, a Table of the Holy Ghost, houses, convents, ramparts with entrance gates, lawns, gardens, water pumps, farms and industrial buildings. The residence of the priest was located outside the beguinage, but sometimes it had a direct entrance too. In general, beguinages never expanded, except for those in Antwerp and Turnhout. If the beguinage was becoming too small, a new beguinage, usually named the 'small beguinage' had to be erected. We will soon examine some typical features of beguinages, such as the exterior of the houses, the gateway, the church and eventually the houses' and convents' interior.

The architectural style differed from court to court. The beguinage of Sint-Truiden was built in a style associated with the Maasland. The beguinages of Hoogstraten and Turnhout were built in a Kempen

---

2.. D'HAENENS, *Begijnhoven van België*, pp. 7 and 9-11.

regional style and those of Aarschot, Antwerp, Diest, Herentals, Leuven, Mechelen and Tienen in a Brabant style. In Antwerp, Hasselt, Tienen, and Tongeren, the houses in the beguinages had a small front garden, separated from the road by a blank wall. Often the houses had a first floor and an outdoor toilet. Before the sixteenth century, the houses were made out of wood and clay and they had a straw roof. More recent houses were made out of sand-stone, ironstone and brick and the roofs were covered with tiles.

Since the seventeenth century, people wanted to show off more, so a lot of attention was paid to the gate building, especially under influence of the Counter Reformation. Diest had one of the most beautiful gates. It was a traditional arch with a monumental and richly sculptured sandstone gate. The basket arch was surrounded by two pillars and the central section contained an inscription of the Song of Songs, viz. *Besloten hof comt in mynen hof myn suster bruyt,* 1671 [*Enclosed Garden, Come into my Garden, my Sister Bride,* 1671]. A niche above the inscription contained a statuette.

The most important building at the beguinage was the church. Some medieval churches have been preserved, for example, the church of St. John the Baptist in Leuven, of St. Catherine in Diest, and that of St. Agnes in Sint-Truiden. The church at Sint-Truiden is especially famous for its wall paintings, dating from around 1300. Two repeated principles were typical for all churches: simplicity and austerity. Usually the

churches did not have a real tower, only a roof-tur-
ret above the choir entrance where the bells hung.
A reduced choir, a nave of considerable length and
broad, heavy side aisles made the place adequate for
a community without choral prayer. All beguines had
their personal seat in the nave. The side aisles were
places for individual prayer. The churches at Diest
and Sint-Truiden were wealthier churches, because
the beguines were richer.

All beguinages received a religious or secular
name, but most frequently the name of a saint. Many
carried the name St. Agnes, because it was widely
believed that she was the founder of the beguine
movement, even before St. Begga was suggested.
Secular names were always related to the geograph-
ical setting (*Ten Wijngaerde* in Bruges and *Ter Hoyen*
in Gent).[3] All houses had their own names – during
the Middle Ages that of the female inhabitant. Since
the sixteenth century they were given saints' names
or biblical names. The names were painted on a plate
and nailed to the door. Other means of identification
were done by placing the saint's statuette in a small
niche above the door, thus enabling people to deduct
the house's name, a feat only possible if they were
able to recognise the saints iconography.

3. GIJSEN, *Vlaamse begijnhoven*, p. 17.

Let us turn to the interiors. At the beguinage, the beguines lived in separate homes and convents. This is an important difference with nuns, who all live together in a cloister. First we will discuss the individual houses, then the convents. Beguines who had sufficient finances could either buy or build a home at the beguinage. The less wealthier beguines could rent one at a low price within a so-called 'convent' or communal house. Only beguines were allowed to buy or build in the court, and even then it was not considered a right of ownership but more a housing right: a *lijf* [life]. Inside the walls, the beguines ruled because they owned all the houses and only their authorities could decide which homes had to be rebuilt or rented. This also meant that a beguine could not rent or rebuild and that her right of ownership ceased if she decided to marry or to abandon beguinehood. Anyone who built or renovated a home acquired one to four *lijven* from the authorities, in proportion to the value of the works that had been carried out.

This meant that the owner of a home acquired the right to choose a certain number of beguines who would be able to enjoy the property for free. Mostly they chose family members or acquaintances. If all the *lijven* were used up, and everyone who owned a *lijf* had died, the beguinage would regain ownership of the home and they could then re-sell or rent it out again. This system was advantageous to both parties. The builder did not have to spend much money, received a free territory, lived for free and enjoyed certain rights. If she decided to leave the court, she could sell those rights thus recovering part of the construction costs. The beguinage acquired funding by selling or renting the homes and income from this was used to maintain the infirmary.

If a beguine wanted to get ownership of a house, this could only be done according to an established procedure. Prices were made known beforehand. The price depended on the size and condition of the houses, what was in it, and the candidate's age. Some beguines had priority, for example beguines who lived within the court were preferred to people from other houses and outsiders. The purchase price could be paid in the form of an annual debt.[4]

In general, the houses were made of brick, the roof of tiles and they had maximum six to eight rooms. There were no precise rules concerning the houses' decoration, but mostly they were sober. For example, it was forbidden to have a bright coloured table-cloth on the table and household furniture had to be simple. The walls could not be papered, but had to be chalked. Worldly scenes could not be depicted. There had to be sober curtains at the windows. The houses had no heating.[5] Beguines were

4. About the legal situation of the houses: F. W. J. KOORN, *Begijnhoven in Holland en Zeeland gedurende de middeleeuwen* (Assen, 1981), pp. 60-77.
5. J. VAN MECHELEN, *Vlaamse begijnhoven: In schemelheyt der maechtlyckheydt* (Brussels, 1973), p. 12.

supposed to treat and maintain their property carefully. Every year the court mistress and the priest visited them to see if repairs were needed. Being women, the beguine had to ask someone else to carry out the work, which had to be completed in six weeks, If this was not done in that timeframe, the court mistress would see that the works were carried out by others at the cost of the resident beguine. A house that could not be maintained because of lack of money would be sold during which time the beguine was given another place to stay. If the inhabitant died, the Grand-mistress visited the house and saw to it that the repairs were carried out before the family could take ownership of the household furniture.

When the number of beguines fell dramatically in the eighteenth century and more and more houses remained empty, the beguinage authorities were forced to rent them out to the laity. Still, the presence of outsiders was not a new phenomenon at the beguinage. Since earlier times, there had been many of them – children were educated there, wealthy beguines' maids and widows rented rooms. With the approval of the court mistress, female family members too could stay at the beguinage.

In contrast to the houses, it was the rule in the 'convents' that several beguines should live together. Of course, such a convent was bigger than a house. Beguines had their own sleeping place, mostly located upstairs. Besides that, there were common rooms, such as a cellar, a kitchen, a workroom, an attic, several parlours, an infirmary and a storage room.

Life in communal houses was similar to life in nunneries. Poorer beguines who lost their house because of lack of money lived in these houses. From the late sixteenth century on, one encountered novices staying in most of the convents all over the area in which they were situated. Most convents were founded by wealthy beguines or clerics. In their statutes, the number of beguines who could reside there for free or at a very cheap prices, were recorded. The founder's inheritance was used to provide certain benefits such as heating, lights, meals. Money was very seldom provided to the beguines in spite of the fact that they had to perform manual labour to support themselves. The number of convents varied from court to court. The beguinage at Leuven had ten such convents, that of Antwerp had three (New Jerusalem, Syon and Saint Barbara or *de Vyf Wondekens*) and that of Diest had four in the seventeenth century (The Convent of the Holy Ghost, the Convent of Calvary, the Convent of Angels and the Convent of the Disciples). Here the naming principle is clearly seen. Earlier beguinages carried the founder's name, but from the sixteenth century a saint or a biblical name had been given. We can deduce the number of beguines in some convents from their names: the Convent of the Holy Ghost for example housed seven beguines, because there are seven gifts of the Holy Ghost.

Besides the general regulations, each convent had its own regulations. The convent mistress read the regulations out loud at regular times, namely on the four Fridays during the Ember days, or the fast days, at the beginning of every new season. All the inhabitants were also required to do devout exercises in memory of the founder. At the convent of St. Barbara in Antwerp for example, the five inhabitants had to say five Paternosters and five Hail Marys every day at nine o'clock in honour of the founder. At noon they had to recite the Psalm *De Profundis* for the sake of the founder's salvation. In exchange, the beguines as a whole, received 50 guilders from the foundation every year.

The every day life of the convent inhabitants was regulated by additional statutes. They lived in a very closed community that did everything together. They went to church in group and returned in group, they went to sleep, got up, prayed and worked at the same hour. These activities took place in common rooms. During the meals, silence had to be kept when the devotional reading was being delivered. A beguine was required at all times to ask permission of the convent mistress if she wanted to make a visit or go out shopping.

Because all beguines had to support themselves, there was no communal cooking in the convents. However sometimes it was required of the younger beguines to prepare meals on a rota-basis for all the convent's inhabitants. It was not uncommon for these young beguines to recieve a small compensation for this work. Beguines in most other convents were normally required to prepare their own meals. The typical beguine cupboard originated here. This large cupboard was divided into separate compartments, in which the beguines put their cutlery and food stocks. Most cupboards had an extension table. All beguines, except the superiors, had to perform certain weekly tasks. Usually, the younger beguines were given the task to wash dishes, do house-cleaning, keep a supply of wood for cooking and heating and sweep the streets of the beguinage. These tasks were organised on a rota.

Normally, a convent mistress was appointed by the court mistresses and the priest in consultation with the inhabitants. She was responsible for the smooth running of the beguinage, the financial controls, the observance of the statutes and the foundation's religious obligations. She had to give account of herself to the court mistress and the priest during their annual visit to the beguinage.

| 2 | Means of Sustenance

Unlike nuns, beguines had to support themselves. Nuns renounced their property when they entered the convent and from that moment on the community supported them. Beguines however, still had rights of ownership and so they were required to support themselves. If a beguine wanted to enter a convent, she had to have enough finances for this purpose, or be in a position to earn suficient to support herself through work. Manual labour was a requirement since beguines were not allowed to spend their time idling. The labour was compatible with the ideals of the *vita apostolica*, which the beguines tried to pursue. This was deemed acceptable as the disciples in Jesus's day also had to support themselves. Work was confined to the beguinage whereever possible, as the movement of the beguines outside the beguinage was restricted.[6]

Even though most of the beguines were supposed to be self-supporting, in practice, this was not the case. After entering the beguinage, they would have to work to subsidise their income. In this way, they ended up with a small income for their work. As beguinages were not taxed and life was kept austere, they were able to enjoy a fair standard of living.

The beguines were involved in many different forms of labour, according to the times and circumstances. Manual labour curbed idleness and improved prayer and spiritual exercise.[7] In the Middle Ages, the beguines specialised in certain branches of the textile industry, rapidly becoming a booming industry in most towns during this period. They worked at carding, spinning, weaving and bleaching. For the

6. VAN AERSCHOT & HEIRMAN, *Flemish Beguinages*, pp. 80-81.
7. MENS, *Oorsprong en betekenis*, p. 75.

bleaching of linen, large amounts of water were required – for this reason many beguinages were situated close to adequate water resources. Beguine products were very cheap and attractive as their labour was cheap and tax-free. Regulations for bleaching prohibited bleaching on Sundays and religious feasts or holydays instituted by the Church. Beguines had to stay on the parcel of land allocated to them, and were not allowed to attend Church in working clothes or to miss mass. During the sixteenth century, the beguinage at Diest built up such a high reputation for their quality of thread, that it became a profitable business. They were forced to expel or fine beguines for violating regulations. Later when the cloth industry became less profitable the beguines occupied themselves with similar female activities, such as the making of bobbin lace, sewing, embroidery, making rosaries and baking communion wafers.

Because the beguines were able to produce goods cheaply they found themselves drawn into disputes with the guilds and corporations who considered the beguine activities to be unfair competition. Beguines were exempted from taxation (*privilegia beguinalia*) and tolls and so avoided the sometimes very rigid rules enforced by the guilds. At one stage, the situation became so bad that angry citizens who protested against these tax and duty exemptions, stormed the beguinage of Sint-Truiden in 1340. In Diest, on the other hand, production was curtailed by the town council to prevent harm to the town's weavers.

During the fifteenth century, in Leuven, the beguinage used child-labour. This undercut the guild's craftworkers. A compromise was called for. After protests in Antwerp in 1576 taxes were levied on beer drunk at the beguinage, where beer could be bought for cheaper prices. Later, even when the beguinages distributed bread out of charity to the poor, the bakers mounted a protest.

Another major source of income was taking care of the ill and weak. This was typical of older beguinages, especially those situated near hospitals. Beguines used to nurse the ill, both within their beguinage and in the outside world. If a beguine became ill, she was taken care of in the beguinage infirmary. Beguines were never allowed to take care of men and/or pregnant women. If a beguine wanted to look after her parents, she had to seek permission from the mistress to leave the court. The 'practical' Joseph II ordained that a beguine was not allowed to leave the patient's home if it was outside the court, until a physician had declared the patient cured. The beguines also made themselves useful by taking care of lepers and sufferers of other common epidemics. Many of the beguines lost their life after contracting fatal illnesses from their patients. During the wars, they looked after casualties, and at the battle of Waterloo beguinages served as hospitals for the civilian and military wounded.

Beguines provided education to earn a living, as well as provide charity to poorer children. Almost all statutes of beguinages contained a clause concerning the education of the children who lived at the beguinage. In 1646, some 250 beguines and 260 children were living in Leuven's beguinage. Many beguines raised one or two children for a small maintenance; other children received board and lodging while attending the beguine school.

All pupils raised in beguinages were raised in accordance with the beguine ideals, which strived to make them exemplary people. They wore doudy and sober clothing and were required to fulfil certain duties. Poorer children were educated for free. The girls had confirmation classes, and were taught to sing and do needlework. Girls were also allowed to spend nights at the beguinage, while the boys were not. Young girls who were aproaching their sixteenth birthday would sometimes be taken into the beguinage to prepare them for a future life as a beguine.

From the nineteenth century public provision of education, particularly for the poor, reduced the need for home tuition by beguine tutors. Their main work now became youth education and care for the weak and sick. The first nursery school in the city of Diest was located at the local beguinage, subsidised by the municipality. In 1849, the Van Humbeeck Law meant the end of the various beguine schools.[8]

8. VAN AERSCHOT & HEIRMAN, *Flemish Beguinages*, pp. 83-84.

| 3 | Religious Life

Before a woman was able to enter a beguinage, she had to go through a trial period, followed by a period of training. It has been estimated that in Diest, during the seventeenth century, the average age of beguines was twenty. In Sint-Truiden, it crept up to twenty-two by the late eighteenth century. In Breda, a postulant had to be at least thirteen years old before she would be accepted into beguinage, while in Leuven the age was twenty.[9] The authorities as well as the priest decided over a person's acceptance; the rules governing this were clearly laid out in the statutes of the movement. It is interesting to note that Hauchinus's statutes for beguines required the following characteristics for women desiring to join the movement: they had to be honest women of good repute, who were not bound by marriage ties or religious vows. They were required to be healthy and without any latent diseases. If these did manifest themselves later, the canditate would be thrown out of the beguinage. During the first three years as a beguine, they were not supported by the movement, so they had to possess necessities such as a bed, linen, clothes and other household accessories. New entrants were required to have someone vouching for them.

9.   Van Mechelen, *Vlaamse begijnhoven*, p. 11.

During their trial period of approximately two years, the so-called novices were required to stay at the convent, where a novice mistress instructed them in the rules, beguine prayers and spirituality. As for the convents, homes for novices had separate rules beside the general ones. These novice houses were formed after the Council of Trent (1545-1563) whose decrees tried to create standards for seminaries to produce highly-educated clerics.

After an initial period of about a year, the novice was required to dress soberly. Following her confession, a ceremony attended by all the beguines, the novice would become a full and true beguine member of the movement and community, and she would now be able to receive beguine privileges. For her initiation, the novice was dressed as a bride, two of the superiors picked her up and and carried her to the altar. A procession of beguines followed them to the church, where they sang the hyms *Veni Creator* and *Oremus*, followed by Mass. After a reading from the Gospel, the priest would ask what the novice bride desired. Her answer would be: 'The mercy of the Lord and union with my fellow sisters'. The priest then granted it to her and the novice was asked if she would persist in the movement. After her confession, the novice took the vows of chastity and obedience. Taking the beguine veil, the priest would bless it, and the two superiors would put it on the novice's head; the priest then put the beguine crown on her head. The ceremonial mass ended with the *Te Deum* and a special blessing. During her confession, the beguine promised to obey the local bishop, the priest responsible for the beguinage, the Grand-mistresses and the statutes of the movement. She also promised that she would live in chastity for as long as she was a beguine. Unlike monks and nuns, she was not required to take vows of poverty or any sacred vows. A festive dinner was held in the court following the confession. Because the celebrations tended to become excessive, bishops took measures to see that they did not last longer than a single day, and only the next-of-kin were invited. Meals were not allowed to be too expensive, and the total number of participants was also limited. No dancing was allowed. When the gates were closed, it signalled the end of the feast and every one had to leave.

During these celebrations and other anniversaries, beguine family members would compose poems to suit the occasion, including an anniversary song and a chronogram, in which all the supposed merits a beguine was meant to have, were praised, often naively. Sometimes these poems were decorated with pious images of saints. Some of the poems had double-entendres (*dubbel rym-geklanck*), as it was possible to read them in two ways, getting a poem with two diametrically-opposite meanings. One example follows:[10]

10. J. VAN BALBERGHE, 'Tweevoudig Rym-Geklanck', *Mechelse bijdragen* 5 (1938) 60.

JOUFF: ANNA CATHARINA VISTERIN
                          die
verfoeijt mits desen   des werelts ijdelheijdt
het Begynen leven   verkiest sy voor altijdt.

Hoort hoe sy laeckt en laet   de Modens ende pracht
heel den Begynen staet   sy voor het beste acht.
etc.

[MISS ANNA CATHARINE VISTERIN
                          who
will from now on detest   the worldly idleness
the beguine life   she prefers forever.

Listen how she condems and omits   fashion and beauty
the whole beguine state   she values more highly
etc.]

The verses could be read from left to right, which resulted in a normal poem. They could also be read from top to bottom where the meaning of the poem was saucy. It was ironic that Anne Catherine in 1796, the recipient of the above poem, gave up her beguine lifestyle after two years, preferring marriage and a life in society.

After her confession, the beguine was allowed to wear the distinct beguine clothing. Initially, there was no uniformity as in religious orders; so each beguinage had its own 'fashion'. In the Middle Ages, beguines dressed as the ordinary middle-class women of the era. This meant that in the first beguinages there was no uniformity of dress, other than that they normally wore grey or blue clothing without jewellery.

It was left to the Grand-mistress to approve the new beguines' clothes. As time progressed, a specific type of habit emerged and by the sixteenth century with a basic style. The colour of the habits became black, a long headscarf was worn and this was tied differently in each beguinage. A veil was also part of a beguine's clothing. After her confession, the new beguine stayed in the novice house for about three years; after this, she received the title to her own home. If there was a shortage of homes, the new beguine stayed in the novice home until housing became available.

The whole beguine rule could be summarised by the *Lied van de Regel* [*Song of the Rule*]:[11]

> Daar is de kerk en daar is het altaar
> En geheel het begijntjes geschaar
> De kerk en 't altaar, het begijntjes geschaar
> De keerse en de kroon, het begijntjes loon
> De wereld en de Bruid, haar eenigen buit
> De refter en de lamp, de schapraaitjes charmant
> De keuken en de vlaaien, de schouwe gelaen
> Werkkamer en cel, het begijntjes gestel
> 't Hof en 't convent, de begijntjes content
> Regel die is
> Hier is de regel, de regel, de regel
> Hier is de regel die zalig is.

> [There is the church and there is the altar
> And the whole community of the beguine
> The Church, the altar, the beguine's community
> The candle and the crown, the beguine's pay

11. Quoted in VAN MECHELEN, *Vlaamse begijnhoven*, p. 16.

The world and the Bridegroom, her ownly booty
The refectory and the lamp, the charming cupboard
The kitchen and the custards, the loaded fireplace
Labour-room and cell, the beguines satisfied
Rule which is
Here's the rule, the rule, the rule,
Here's the rule, which is beatific.]

Or by this acrostichon from a treatise about
beguine life in Middle Dutch:[12]

B = bruid des Heren [*bride of the Lord*]
E = eenvoud [*simplicity*]
G = goedertierenheid [*benevolence*]
Y = innigheid ten opzichte van God en de heiligen
        [*intimacy towards God and the saints*]
N = nederigheid [*humility*]

Austerity was the norm, requiring the hair to be cut
short, while clothes were to be made of simple
undyed fabrics, sometimes of rabbit or cat skin.
Clothes were not to be overly starched, and a mini-
mum number of hairpins were to be used for fixing
the headscarf. The sleeves of the habits were stitched
up to the hands, and precautions were taken to make
sure that clothes were unable to be blown open by
the wind. Similarly shoes were plain and had no buck-
les or laces. Only black strawhats without trimmings
were allowed. In 1759, the beguines of the *Klein
Begijnhof* of Brussels complained to a visitor that
young girls no longer wanted to enter the movement
because the clothing was too drab.

12. VERACHTERT, *Voorsale des hemels*, p. 36.

The obligations required of the beguines are made clear when one studies the statutes. Their daily obligations were the attendance of Holy Mass and the praying of the lesser offices of Our Lady and the Seven Witnesses. Illiterates had to say the Lord's Prayer and Hail Marys. People in convents were required by the founder to do prescribed religious exercises, as well as obligatory prayers. On Sundays and Holy days, they had other obligations apart from Mass, such as attending sermons, evening choir, Compline and Lauds. Important Holy days of the church, the Feast of the Dedication of their church and their patron saint's anniversary were also obligatory. Some regions had their own local practices; for example in Diest, the beguines had to make the sign of the cross and say a prayer to the Holy Spirit every time the bells chimed. Beguines had to take part in processions and solemn invocations. Many Grand-mistresses disliked these activities, because they were followed by fairs and other forms of entertainment. At the beguinage of Antwerp, there was a list of processions beguines were not allowed to participate in under any circumstances. In some places, processions were held at the court itself, and these can still be seen in Turnhout (the only difference being that there are now no beguines in these ceremonies).

In and on both the beguinages and the houses, the crucifixion and saints are regularly depicted, illustrating that the devotional aspect of the beguines centred on worshipping the suffering Christ and participating in the mass. The beguines also had a lively devotion to Our Lady and other so-called virgin saints such as Catherine of Alexandria (recognised by the church as the beguines' patron saint), Begga (recognised as fellow patron saint), Elisabeth of Hungary (who was concerned for the sick), Mary Magdalene and Veronica (who experienced the Lord's suffering from very close), Anna (patron saint of weavers), Agnes (who refused to marry because she had taken the Lord as her bridegroom), Barbara (saint for urgent needs) and Catherine of Siena (a mystic, who was stigmatised). Saints who were only venerated in a few towns, were often revered in the beguinages of those towns, e.g. St. Denys in Diest and Blessed Gertrude of Oosten in Antwerp.

In order to maintain silent solitude, every beguinage was cut off from the outside world by high walls with at least one gate, a female porter keeping watch. The statutes contained measures against noise-makers. During meals and after the ringing of the evening bell, total silence was proclaimed and observed. At other times, only quiet speaking was allowed, preferably about religious subjects. Beguines who were shown to have broken this rule, were punished. At some beguinages, the severest punishment involved whipping.[13]

Iconographic and literary means were used to prevent the beguines from leaving the beguinage.

13. VAN MECHELEN, *Vlaamse begijnhoven*, p. 11.

Through numerous small paintings, Jesus was depicted as warning a beguine against marriage. There is a legend about the beguinage at Sint-Truiden that is worth mentioning. There lived a beguine from Alsteren who was seduced by a young man. While he was waiting for her in a cemetery one evening in 1493, suddenly nine corpses raised themselves from their graves and walked towards the convent. As a result he was convinced that a religious life was better than marriage and he subsequently entered a monastery. Leaving a beguinage was unpardonable, and caused a beguine the loss of her housing rights. This even applied if she chose to enter a nunnery.

Beguines who fell ill were taken care of in the convent or in their own house. If she did not recover, or was unable to care for herself, she could go to the beguinage infirmary where she would be looked after for the rest of her life or until she recovered. If the Last Rites were to be administered, all the beguines followed the Blessed Sacrament in procession to the sick woman's house. Four of them carried the *Baldaquin* and four others carried processional lanterns, while the others followed praying. In the case of death, all court inhabitants were obliged to visit the deceased and to pray for her salvation. The deceased was laid out wearing her best habit and her confessional crown. The type of funeral depended on her status. At most beguinages, it was habitual to distribute bread to the court's inhabitants and to family members and acquaintances. Because beguinages were parishes in their own right, they had their own cemeteries. The burial-place was determined by the status of the deceased, the rich being interned within the chuch, while the others were buried in the adjacent cemetery.[14]

| 4 | The Organisation of the Beguinage

Beguinages did not have a central building or central administration as in religious houses. However, they were autonomous and had their own authorities and statutes.[15] These could be different from court to court. Because most beguinages adopted common statutes, this brought about affiliations in beguinage statutes. In the beginning the statutes were handed down by mouth, and only the important ones were written down. From the fourteenth century, everything was in writing.[16] In most cases these statutes were formulated by the founder of the beguinage after being approved of by the local bishop.[17] The statutes regulated the entire organisation and administration of the beguinage. The rule of Monsignor

14. On beguinage life in general: VAN AERSCHOT & HEIRMAN, *Flemish Beguinages*, pp. 55-92.
15. Unless otherwise mentioned, this section is based on TROOSKENS, 'Begijnen', pp. 61-72.
16. KOORN, *Begijnhoven*, pp. 37-38.
17. R. BOUDENS, *De kerk in Vlaanderen: Momentopnamen*, Averbode, 1994, p. 57.

Hauchinus contained the main principles:[18]

Van die conditien der Persoonen die men sal aenveerden totten Beggijnhove
  [about the candidates' conditions of acceptance]
Van het aenveerden en Beloften der Beggijnkens
  [about the conditions of acceptance and the beguines' vows]
Vant Habijt ende Huysraet der Beggijnkens
  [about the beguine habit and their household goods]
Van den Dienst Godts, ende het Bidden der Beggijnen, ende hoe sij de H.H. Sacramenten des Aulthaers en Biechten gebruycken sullen [about religious duties]
Vande conversatie ende handelinghe der Beggijnkens
  [rules about behaviour and speech]
Vande Poortieressen, uyt ende ingaen der Beggijnen
  [rules for the female porters and rules about entering and leaving the court]
Vande Beggijntiens Correctie [about disciplinary measures]
Vande Priesters des Hofs [rules for the priest of the beguinage]
Vanden Huysen des Beggijnhofs, diemen coopt en vercoopt
  [about the buying and selling of houses]
Vanden gemeyne huysen en conventen des Hofs
  [communal houses and convents]
Vande Infirmerie ende H. Geest Huysen
  [about the infirmary and the houses of the Holy Ghost]
Vande Overheyt des Beggijn-hofs
  [about the beguinage's administration]

We will discuss the aspects about the beguinage's administration in the following order. Its Church and its Officers, the infirmary and the Table of the holy Ghost. At the head of the beguinage were one or sev-

18. Quoted in VAN MECHELEN, *Vlaamse begijnhoven*, p. 11.

eral *magistrae* or *meestersen* [mistresses], a rector who gave spiritual guidance, normally a priest or pastor, and custodians who cared for practical matters.

The number of mistresses varied according to the area that the beguinage covered. This was fixed in the statutes. The larger beguinages had four. The name given to the most important mistress could differ from court to court, but one mostly spoke of the Grandlady or Grand-mistress. She took care of the daily administration and decided who would be postulants. She gave out punishments when due, visited the court, sold and rented houses, guarded the peace and protected the court's rights against outsiders. Mostly a court mistress was elected and could be re-elected. In Belgium and the Southern Netherlands, it was often customary that Grand-mistresses were appointed by the founder of the beguinage or his heirs, instead of being elected.[19] Court mistresses generally had to be over forty. It was important that they had been living at the beguinage for over ten years. An elected mistress got an official residence, which was larger than the other houses. In her house she kept a chest containing all important records and documents that concerned the beguinage. Mistresses were recognised by their head-dress. The the headdress of each beguinage was different.

From the fourteenth century onwards, the beguinage priests were secular clerics who had offered

19. KOORN, *Begijnhoven*, p. 41.

spiritual guidance to the community as rectors. The priest's rights and duties differed from court to court. His most important task was the beguines' spiritual care. His most important duty was the spiritual well-being of the beguines, daily mass, Sunday mass, and the principal mass on Holy days. He was required to deliver sermons, take confession, administer Holy Communion and the Last Rites. In most beguinages he was also part of the administration. He was entitled a house that was free of costs and taxes. Because men were not allowed to live in the court, his house was built against the exterior wall of the beguinage. If there was enough money, the priest was allowed to ask for the assistance of a chaplain. The clerics were assisted by a female sacristan. She was a beguine who maintained the church and prepared mass. She also decorated the church, washed the liturgical garments and served at the altar carrying the wine and bread for mass.[20]

The infirmary was, after the church, the most important and often oldest institution at the beguinage.[21] Infirmaries were hospitals or hospices (the secular word of that time) for elderly beguines or lodgers. It usually had its own chapel and chap-

20. *Ibid.*, p. 51.
21. Very often it is the oldest institution, because in some Belgian towns the infimery existed before the beguinages. It could happen that beguines started living next to an infirmery, so that a beguine community arose that later became a beguinage (KOORN, *Begijnhoven*, p. 52).

lain. Taking care of the ill was the chaplain's most important task, although spiritual care was also a priority. Sometimes, needy beguines stayed at the infirmary. So would visitors (clerics or family members) who were allowed to spend the night. As in the court, laziness was not tolerated in the infirmary. Days were spent praying and doing handiwork.

The Table of the Holy Ghost, which could be found in all towns during that era, was the beguinage's charitable institution. Poor beguines who were unable to support themselves, could appeal to the Table of the Holy Ghost. In exchange for support, the beguines had to donate their furniture and property to the institution. The head of the Holy Ghost Table, was also one of the beguinage's convent mistresses. In promoting the temporary interests of the beguinage, convent mistresses were supported by *momboren, procuratores* or *begijnenmeesters* [guardians]. These were laymen or clerics who were occupied mostly with managing the court's possessions and with representing the beguinage in judicial conflicts. During the Ancien Régime, women did not possess corporate rights and had to be represented by guardians. Married women were represented by their husbands. Unmarried women could choose their custodian.[22] As members of a beguinage, they had the same rights as beguines.

22. KOORN, *Begijnhoven*, p. 44.

| IV |
THE THIRTEEN BEGUINAGES
GRANTED WORLD HERITAGE STATUS

This is a short overview of the thirteen Belgian beguinages that are recognised as World Heritage Sites by UNESCO.[1]

| 1 | **Bruges**

History

The beguinage of Bruges was founded in 1244. Afterwards, the Countess of Flanders, Margaretha of Constantinople, and the Bishop of Tournai, Walter of Marvis, changed it into an autonomous parish, called 'De Wijngaard' [the Vineyard]. During the religious reformations of the sixteenth century, it served as a refuge and farmers used the church as a haybarn. In 1584, a fallen candle caused the church, which was dedicated to St. Elisabeth, to burn down. It was rebuilt in 1605. On the outside the building is austere. The interior is in a late Baroque style. During

1. On the history of recognition: VAN AERSCHOT & HEIRMAN, *Flemish Beguinages*, pp. 141-184.

the French Revolution, the beguine movement was condemned and the beguines had to leave. They could not return until 1803. During the First World War, the beguinage again served as a refuge. In 1927, it became a monastery for Benedictine sisters. They still live there now and dress as beguines.

Points and objects of interest

The beguinage of Bruges is a typical example of a courtyard beguinage. Most houses date from the fifteenth, sixteenth or seventeenth century and many of the original ones have been preserved. The houses are centred around a green park with trees. The gateway, built in Classical style, is dated from 1776. The earlier church, destroyed in a fire, was rebuilt in 1605. During the restoration in 1991, some remarkable wall paintings were discovered. In the beguinage, there is a Beguine Museum, a liturgical centre, a guest-wing and a room for quiet prayer.

Bibliography

F. BONNEURE & L. VERSTRAETE, *Het prinselijk begijnhof De Wijngaard te Brugge: Geschiedenis van de site en van de bewoners* (Tielt, 1992); C. CALLEWAERT, *Les plus anciens documents des archives du béguinage de Bruges*, Handelingen van het Genootschap voor Geschiedenis gesticht onder de benaming Société d'Emulation te Brugge, 54 (Bruges, 1904); D. DESMET, *Het begijnhof De Wijngaard te Brugge: Onderzoek naar het dagelijks leven rond het midden van de vijftiende eeuw* [unpublished master's dissertation Katholieke Universiteit Leuven] (Leuven, 1979); E. DHONDT, *Geschiedenis van het Begijnhof te Brugge vanaf zijn ontstaan tot het einde van de 13de eeuw* [unpublished master's dissertation Katholieke Universiteit Leuven] (Leuven, 1964); R. HOORNAERT, *Le Béguinage Princier de Bruges: Le Passé, le Présent* (Bruges, 1938); IDEM, *Le Béguinage de Bruges, son histoire, sa règle, sa vie* (Bruges, 1930) [English version: *The Beguinage of Bruges: The Vineyard Then and Now* (Ostend, 1988)]; IDEM, *La plus ancienne règle du béguinage de Bruges* (Bruges, 1930) ; H. VRIELYNCK, *Brugsche Begijnhoflegende rond Memlinc* (Bruges, 1939).

| 2 | Dendermonde

History

Dendermonde once had two beguinages, both dedicated to St. Alex. The first was founded in 1223. However, as it was built on a marsh, it disappeared. In 1289, the Bishop of Cambrai ordered a new beguinage to be built. This is the present beguinage situated on the riverbank. After the restrictions enforced by the Council of Vienne, Robert de Béthune ('the Lion of Flanders') attempted to mediate. This beguinage also suffered during the Reformation. From this time onwards, the strength of this community decreased. Most houses were rebuilt in the seventeenth century. The French Revolution caused the closure of the Dendermonde church, and the beguines were forcibly laicised. In 1865, the Liberal government of Belgium sold the beguinage to Baron Frederic-Charles van der Brugghen-de Nayer. He rented it back to the Grand-mistress. In 1975, the last beguine of Dendermonde, also the beguinage's last Grand-mistress, Ernestine De Bruyne, died.

Points and objects of interest

The beguinage's church dates from 1928 and is built in Neo-Gothic style. It replaced a sixteenth-century building destroyed in the First World War. Now there are two museums at the beguinage: the Beguine Museum and the Museum of Folklore.

Bibliography

J. BROECKAERT, *Cartularium van het Begijnhof van Dender-monde, voorafgegaan van eene historische schets dezes gestichts* (Dendermonde, 1902); G. DE COSTER, *Het begijnhof van Dendermonde vanuit institutioneel oogpunt* [unpublished master's dissertation Katholieke Universiteit Leuven] (Leuven, 1991); A. STROOBANTS et al., *700 jaar Begijnhof (1288-1988)* (Dendermonde, 1988).

| 3 | Diest

History

The oldest document in which the St. Elisabeth beguinage is mentioned, dates from 1253 when Arnold VI, Lord of Diest, had the church built. It had the same appearance as in the seventeenth century. It is still a village in the form of a P, with four streets. In 1687, 282 beguines were living in the beguinage's

99 houses. The movement was most successful then. In 1833, 62 beguines lived in the beguinage, and in 1928 the last two left. The houses are made of red brick. White sandstone was used for the important houses. Every house has a niche above the door, containing a saint or a sculpture. The church was built in the fourteenth century. Over time it acquired some beautiful furnishing. It is now in urgent need of renovation.

So far only the houses have been restored and the infirmary was turned into a cultural centre. The beautiful gateway was built in Baroque style in 1671. The beguinage contains an art gallery, named after the second founder of the beguinage, Nicolaes Esschius.

Points and objects of interest

Today, the beguinage is a hive of commercial activity. Apart from the cultural centre and the art gallery, the former Convent of the Holy Ghost is now a restaurant serving traditional Flemish cuisine. The Beguine Museum, which once existed in the Angel's Convent is no longer operational. Today, the houses serve as accommodation for artists, art-shops, bookbinders and other craft activities.

Bibliography

Diest 1900: Beschrijving van de parochie van St. Catharina (begijnhof), beschrijving van de parochie van St. Sulpitius, beschrijving van de parochie van O.-L.-Vrouw (Wespelaar,

1989); A. ELST, *Het Diestse begijnhof: wereldcultuurmonument* (Diest, 1999); M. LEMMENS, *Het begijnhof te Diest (ca. 1245-ca. 1400)* [unpublished master's dissertation Katholieke Universiteit Leuven] (Leuven, 1987); L.J.M. PHILIPPEN, 'Het begijnhof van S.-Catharina "ten Velde" te Diest', *Bijdragen tot de Geschiedenis* 3 (1904) 501-519; 4 (1905) 327-339, 423-433 and 532-536; L. STROOBANT, 'Le Béguinage de Diest', *Folklore Brabançon* 20 (1940-8) 226-227; M. VAN DER EYCKEN, 'Nicolaas van Essche en de hervorming van het Diestse Begijnhof', *Arca Lovaniensis* 5 (1976) 277-297; R. VAN DE VEN, 'Een inventaris van de infirmerie van het begijnhof te Diest (1636)', *Oost-Brabant* 16 (1979) 33-39. R. WECKX, 'Begijnen en begijnenbeweging te Diest tot 1325 (I+II)', *Eigen schoon & De Brabander* 86 (2003) 231-250 and 367-380.

| 4 | Gent

History

Gent had several beguinages. The old St. Elisabeth beguinage, founded around 1235, lost something of its original character due to poor restoration. The beguines left their houses and convents in 1874 and settled in Sint-Amandsberg (near Gent), which is a rare example of a nineteenth-century beguinage. The most interesting beguinage in Gent is the so-called *Klein Begijnhof* or Small Beguinage, dedicated to Our Lady 'of the Hay'. It was founded by Joanne of Constantinople around 1240 and was situated between the third and fourth city walls. In 1815, the beguines took care of war victims after the battle of

Waterloo. In 1832 they looked after people who suffered from cholera. The beguinage was sold in 1867 and was purchased by the Duke of Arenberg, who protected it from dereliction. Today it is a centre for disabled children, and a religious and architectural institution. Most of the houses are inhabited by students, young families and elderly people. Other buildings, mostly the convents, are used as library or documentation centres.

Points and objects of interest

The *Klein Begijnhof* of Gent is a perfect example of a courtyard beguinage, surrounded by a green common, houses, convents, the infirmary and the church. Several houses have disappeared, the most famous being the Plague House and the brewery. It is interesting to pay a visit to the house of the Great Mistress, built in 1661. This house contains precious furniture and paintings. Also worth visiting are the chapels of the Holy Grave and Saint Godeliph and the farm with its old hay tower.

Bibliography

J. BETHUNE, *Cartulaire du Béguinage Sainte-Elisabeth à Gand* (Bruges, 1883); J.P. DE PUE, *Geschiedenis van het Groot Begijnhof Sint-Elisabeth Gent en St. Amandsberg* (Leuven, 1984); H. GAILLIAU, *Soo geluckigh als een beggijn: Het begijnhof O.L.V. ter Hooie te Gent (1584-1792)* [unpublished master's dissertation Katholieke Universiteit Leuven] (Leuven, 1992); R. HAESERYN, 'De tentoonstelling "Iconografie van het oude

Sint-Elisabethbegijnhof te Gent"', *Oostvlaamse Zanten* 47 (1972) 19-22; G. HENDRIX & J. HENDRIX, *Onze Lieve Vrouw Ter Hoyen, hortus conclusus van Clausynne Vandennieuwelande,* Documenta libraria, 26 (Leuven, 2001); G. HENDRIX, *Steedsels in het Gents begijnhof Onze Lieve Vrouw Ter Hoyen 1627-1953: Facsimile-editie van de steedselboeken met inleiding en begijnenregister,* Begijnhofpublicaties, 1-2 (Gent, 2001); IDEM, *Het beproevingsvol- begenadigde leven van begijntje Coleta De Groote (1791-1816), geestelijke dochter van Petrus Theodoor Verhaegen, voorlaatste rector magnificus van de aloude universiteit van Leuven,* Documenta libraria, 26 (Leuven, 2001); L. JOOS, *Begijnhof O.L. Vrouw ter Hoye: Geschiedenis en gids* (Gent, 1934); F. VAN BOST, 'Ontdek het Begijnhof en uw Heem. Gent', *Oostvlaamse Zanten* 38 (1963) 278-279; C. VANDENBUSSCHE, 'Bijdrage tot de bouwgeschiedenis van het Sint-Elisabethbegijnhof te Gent', *Kultureel Jaarboek Oost-Vlaanderen* (1970) 231-257; P.WELVAERT, '1617-1797: 180 jaar wonen in het Sint-Elisabethbegijnhof te Gent', *Bijdragen tot de Geschiedenis* (1980) 219-266; *Werken en kerken: 750 jaar begijnhofleven te Gent* (Gent, 1984). General: G. CELIS, 'Tentoonstelling der begijnhoven te Gent', *Vandaag Brussel* 1 (1929) 314-320 and A. WYFFELS, 'De moeilijkheden rond de Gentse begijnhoven op het einde van de 18de en in de 19de eeuw', *Oostvlaamse Zanten* 45 (1970) 164-175.

| 5 | Hoogstraten

History

The Our Lady beguinage of Hoogstraten was probably founded in the second half of the fourteenth century. This is when it is first mentioned. In that year John of Cuyck, Lord of Hoogstraten, gave permission to build a church for the beguines. In 1436, the beguinage became an autonomous parish with a few inhabitants. During the period of the Wars of Religion many beguines from elsewhere took refuge in the comparative safety of the Hoogstraten beguinage. In the seventeenth century, the number of beguines increased remarkably. In the twentieth century, their number decreased and many houses became state property. In 1971, the complete beguinage was declared a conservation area. One year later, in 1972, the last beguine died. In 1997, the beguinage was renovated and won the 'Flemish Monument Prize' and in 1998 it got the title of 'Laureate of the Henry Ford European Conservation Award'. The houses are gathered round two square inner courtyards, one of which is larger than the other.

Points and objects of interest

The original church dates from 1388 and was replaced by the present Baroque church in 1680. It is extraordinarily rich and contains many treasures and furniture. The beguinage has an art museum with the works of the famous Belgian artist Alfred Ost (1884-1945). It also has an urban museum.

Bibliography

R. LAMBRECHTS, 'Het Begijnhof van Hoogstraten (1380-1600)', *Hoogstratense Oudheidkundige Kring* 27 (1959) v-xx and 21-204 [= published version of unpublished master's dissertation Katholieke Universiteit Leuven, 1958]; J. LAUWERYS, *Het begijnhof van Hoogstraten*, Jaarboek van de Koninklijke Hoogstratense Oudheidkundige Kring, 1974-1976 (Hoogstraten, 1976).

| 6 | Kortrijk

History

The beguinage of Kortrijk, dedicated to St. Elisabeth, is classed as a model village. It has little cobblestone streets, many dwarf hedges and 41 houses with Baroque façades. Unlike other beguinages, Kortrijk lies inside the city walls, next to the city centre. It stands between the Church of Our Lady and that of St. Martin. It was a gift of Joanne of Flanders, Countess of Flanders, in 1238. In 1250, the beguinage statutes were written. The beguinage was destroyed in 1302 during the famous Battle of Kortrijk (or the Battle of the Golden Spurs) between France and Flanders. In the fourteenth century, the houses and church were renovated and beguine life in Kortrijk reached a peak of popularity in the seventeenth century. In 1788, 400 French soldiers were housed in the military hospital established at the beguinage. Afterwards, empty houses were rented out to towns-people, but gradually the beguines were able to regain their property. In 1853, they opened a school for forty girls which later turned into a school for the poor.

Points and objects of interest

In 1875, many houses were dismantled to enlarge the central street of the beguinage. Nevertheless, the cobbled streets and many seventeenth century houses still remain today. The Grand-mistress lived in the largest house. It was she who ruled over the beguinage. Her house had a crow-stepped gable and a 'great hall' and can still be visited today. The beguinage has its own Beguine Museum. The chapel was consecrated in 1464. A few fifteenth century houses have survived.

Bibliography

J. DE CUYPER, 'Het begijnhof van Kortrijk. Ontstaan en oudste periode', *De Leiegouw* 15 (1973); R. MATTELAAR, 'Straatjes, beluiken, hoven, koeren, reken en partjes te Kortrijk', *Biekorf* 80 (1980) 45-54.

| 7 | Lier

History

The beguinage of Lier, immortalised in the works of Felix Timmermans, is one of the best preserved beguinages in the country. It was founded in the thirteenth century outside the city walls near a river and it became a parish in 1259. It has a troubled history. The beguinage was constantly struggling with the collegiate church of St. Gummarus of Lier, while in several other disasters (in 1485, 1526 and 1542), parts of the beguinage were destroyed. In the Napoleonic period, when two hundred beguines had been resident, the beguinage was sold off to private individuals and the church became a Temple of the Law. In the nineteenth century the beguines returned, but today, only private persons (such as artists and craftworkers) live at the beguinage. That is in strong contrast with the situation that existed in the fourteenth century when 300 beguines were living in the 162 small houses. The last beguine, Sister Agnes, died in 1994.

Points and objects of interest

The square beguinage has eleven streets and has been carefully restored. The novices' convent is probably the most remarkable extant example. The church, dedicated to St. Margaret of Antioch, was rebuilt in 1664 and is a beautiful example of the Flemish Renaissance style. It is filled with magnificent Baroque art. A little chapel with an *ecce homo* sculpture is attached to the church wall. Another place of interest is the Calvary.

Bibliography

K. BIERMANS, *Het begijnhof te Lier* (Antwerp, 1948); P.J. GOETSCHALCKX, 'Het begijnhof van Lier, oorkonden', *Bijdragen tot de Geschiedenis* 3 (1904) 36-56; Kunstkring Konvent (ed.), *Het Liers begijnhof: Artiestenoord en inspiratiebron* (Lier, 1978).

17. Sculpture of St. Begga (s. XVII).
Herentals, Begijnhofmuseum (*Copyright IRPA-KIK Brussel*)

18. Jan Verhoeven, St. Begga as patron saint of beguines
and beghards (c. 1641-1660).
Mechelen, Church of the beguinage
(Copyright IRPA-KIK Brussel)

19. Louis Tytgadt, After a Service in the Small Beguinage of Gent (1890). Gent, Museum voor Schone Kunsten *(Copyright IRPA-KIK Brussel)*

20. Ferdinand Willaert († 1938), Beguinage of Mechelen.
Brugge, Groeningemuseum *(Copyright IRPA-KIK Brussel)*

21. Bernard De Pooter, Beguinage of Turnhout (1926).
Turnhout, Taxandriamuseum – TRAM 41
(Copyright IRPA-KIK Brussel)

22. Sint-Amandsberg. Needlework and embroidery (c. 1920)

23. Sint-Amandsberg. Bleaching of the linen (c. 1920)

24. Gent. Small Beguinage. Ceremony with beguines
(early twentieth century)

| 8 | Leuven

History

The *Groot Begijnhof* of Leuven is first mentioned in a document dating from 1232 in which the authorities gave their permission for the building of a new chapel for the city's pious women. The beguinage was built between the first and the second city walls and is, as is the case in Lier and Diest, a little town in the much larger city. It was a very large beguinage (having four court mistresses once) and it was probably the most frequently visited beguinage along with that of Bruges. In Leuven you can clearly see that the beguinage is a town within the city, because the beguinage is cut in two by a river and the houses are all different in size. In the flourishing seventeenth century, three hundred beguines were living in the houses and the convents. At the end of the 1950s the buildings were to be demolished, but fortunately the university was looking for a place to house students and staff and purchased it. The restoration of the buildings took thirty years.

We should not entirely forget the *Klein Begijnhof* on the opposite side of the city, founded in 1275. It consists of only one street with seventeenth- and eighteenth-century houses, all inhabited by private individuals.

Points and objects of interest

The church dedicated to St. John the Baptist is worth visiting. One of its former priests was Pope Adrian VI (1522-1523). Two memorial stones are located in the porch and are inscribed with the dates 1234 and 1305. They refer to the establishment of the beguinage. The austere building fits with the lifestyle of the early beguines, but the interior proves that the people wanted to show their wealth during the age of the Counter-Reformation. In the church, the visitor has to walk over the gravestones of ninety beguines and priests buried between 1396 and 1753.

Bibliography

J. DE KEMPENEER, 'Een kanonieke visitatie van het Leuvens Groot-Begijnhof in 1665', *Journal des Petites Affiches: Hebdomadaire de l'arrondissement de Louvain* 150 (1968) 14-20; R.M. LEMAIRE, L.F. GÉNICOT, R. VAN THIELEN, & A.MATHIJS, 'L'infirmerie du Grand Béguinage de Louvain', *Bulletin van de Koninklijke Commissie voor Monumenten en Landschappen* 16 (1965-66); W.A. OLYSLAGER, *Het Groot Begijnhof van Leuven* (Leuven, 1973); R. UYTTERHOEVEN, *Het Groot Begijnhof van Leuven* (Leuven, 1996) [translated in English]. The small beguinage: A. STRUYF, 'De konventen van de infirmerij van het klein begijnhof te Leuven', *Mededelingen van de Geschied- en Oudheidkundige Kring voor Leuven en Omgeving* 4 (1964) 73-96.

| 9 | Mechelen

History

In 1259, the Bishop of Cambrai gave permission to the heir and to the beguines who were living scattered over the town of Mechelen to go and live together outside the city. They settled and founded the *Groot Begijnhof* of Mechelen in the year 1500. At that time, some 1800 beguines were living in 99 convents. Some of the older, incapacitated beguines refused to move and decided to live near St. Catherine's church. This community became known as the *domus debilium beghinarum*, and in 1562 was renamed the *Klein Begijnhof*. In 1822, it became a primary school. Nowadays, there is very little left of the buildings, having been plundered and sacked several times during the Wars of Religion. In 1577 it was completely destroyed and 1200 beguines and 300 laymen were forced to leave. The beguines had to settle somewhere else in the city in what is now the *Groot Begijnhof*. Their statutes were also composed by bishop Hauchinus.

Points and objects of interest

The beguine church of Mechelen is a typical Baroque church, dedicated to Ss. Alex and Catherine, and completed by Lucas Fayd'herbe. It contains works by Cossiers, Fayd'herbe, Duquesnoy and Franchoys. The two houses that belonged to the Grand-mistress (the houses Alex and Ambrose) as well as several convents in the court are worth visiting.

Bibliography

Begijnhof Mechelen 1973 (Mechelen, 1973); C.B. DE RIDDER, 'Documents concernant les béguines de Mechelen et d'Aarschot', *Analectes pour servir à l'histoire ecclésiastique de Belgique* 11 (1875) 22-34 ; F. DE RIDDER, 'Het altaar van de huurkapellen op het voormalige Begijnhof te Mechelen', *Handelingen van de Koninklijke Kring voor Oudheidkunde, Letteren en Kunst van Mechelen* 36 (1931) 42-48; IDEM, 'De Conventen van het Oud Begijnhof te Mechelen', *Handelingen van de Koninklijke Kring voor Oudheidkunde, Letteren en Kunst van Mechelen* 42 (1937) 22-83; IDEM, 'De geestelijkheid van het oude Mechelse Begijnhof', *Handelingen van de Koninklijke Kring voor Oudheidkunde, Letteren en Kunst van Mechelen* 44 (1939) 17-48; IDEM, 'Mechelens Groot-Begijnhof binnen de stad', *Handelingen van de Koninklijke Kring voor Oudheidkunde, Letteren en Kunst van Mechelen* 40 (1935) 15-43; IDEM, 'De oorsprong van het Mechels Begijnhof en van de parochies in de volkswijk der stad tijdens de XIIIde en XIVde eeuw', *Handelingen van de Koninklijke Kring voor Oudheidkunde, Letteren en Kunst van Mechelen* 35 (1930) 56-84; IDEM, 'De oudste statuten van het Mechelsche Begijnhof', *Handelingen van de Koninklijke Kring voor Oudheidkunde, Letteren en Kunst van Mechelen* 39 (1934) 18-29; IDEM, 'Rekening van de maaltijd, gegeven ter gelegenheid van de kerkwijding op het Groot Begijnhof te Mechelen (8 september 1647)', *Handelingen van de Koninklijke Kring voor Oudheidkunde, Letteren en Kunst van Mechelen* 45 (1940) 99-102; L.J.M. PHILIPPEN, 'Begijnenwerkzaamheden, naar een schilderij in 't Mechels begijnhof', *P. Verheyden gehuldigd* (Antwerp, 1943) pp. 51-70; R.TAMBUYSER, 'Het oud archief van het Oud Begijnhof van Mechelen', *Handelingen van de Koninklijke Kring voor Oudheidkunde, Letteren en Kunst van Mechelen* 60 (1955) 25-50 and 61 (1956), 44-49; R. VAN AERDE, 'Het Elisabeth van Nerim Convent gesticht 1564 op het Oude Groot Begijnhof van Mechelen', *Mechelse Bijdragen* 8 (1941) 1-18; J. VAN BALBERGHE, 'Tweevoudig Rym-Geklanck bij de Plechtige steding eener Mechelse begyn', *Mechelse Bijdragen* 5 (1938) 59-64; S. VANDENBERGHE, '16de-eeuwse begijnen-woningen op het Groot Begijnhof te Mechelen', *Handelingen van de Koninklijke Kring voor Oudheidkunde van Mechelen* 90 (1976) 158-169; C. VAN DE WIEL, 'De begijnhoven en de vrouwelijke gemeenschappen in het aartsbisdom Mechelen', *Ons Geestelijk Erf* 43 (1970) 152-212; 44 (1971) 179-214 and 45 (1972) 278-344 and 369-428; A. VAN DEN EYNDEN, *Statuten der begijnhoven van Mechelen, Brugge en het bisdom Luik (13de eeuw)* [unpublished master's dissertation Katholieke Universiteilt Leuven] (Leuven, 1960); F. VERMUYTEN, *Het begijnhof van Mechelen en zijn kerk* (Antwerp, 1971).

| 10 | Sint-Amandsberg (near Gent)

History

The beguinage of Sint-Amandsberg is the most recent one in Belgium. Its roots lay in the troubles that beguines met with in Gent, caused by the French, Dutch and Belgian authorities. During the French Revolution, the beguines had lost their property and though they were later allowed to return during the period when the Belgian and Dutch provinces were united (1815-30), new problems would arise when

Belgium became independent. When the Liberals won the municipal elections of 1858, the beguines became the victims of the conflict between Liberal and Catholic politicians. The Liberals wanted the beguine houses to be reserved for poor people and undertook a reform of the beguinages. The 700 beguines were forced to move into an area that was especially bought for this purpose by the Duke of Arenberg. Arthur Verhaegen designed the buildings and Baron de Béthune (a famous Neo-Gothic revivalist) built the church. The works started in 1873 and one year later the first beguines moved into the completed buildings.

Points and objects of interest

The Neogothic church, the house of the Grand-mistress and the museum in St. Julian's House are open to visitors.

Bibliography

A. BOEN, *Wat zijn de begijntjes?* (Sint-Amandsberg, 1928); *100 jaar Mont Saint Amand. Avonden in het begijnhof* (Sint-Amandsberg, 1972); L. LUYTS, *Het Groot Begijnhof van Sint-Elizabeth in zijn verleden en heden* (Sint-Amandsberg, 1965); R. POELMAN, *125 jaar Groot Begijnhof te Mont Saint Amand (1874-1999)* (Gent, 1999); A. RUTTEN, *Begijntjesleven: Het groot-hof van St. Amandsberg* (Gent, 1922); IDEM, *Dans le béguinage* (s.l., 1910); *Une visite au Béguinage Ste Elisabeth à Mont-St.-Amand-lez-Gand* (Gent, 1928).

| 11 | Sint-Truiden

History

The documents of foundation of the St. Agnes beguinage of Sint-Truiden were signed by Abbot William of Ryckel in 1265 and confirmed by Pope Clement IV two years later. They were meant to put an end to the spread of unenclosed beguines. The beguinage was built outside the city walls near the Cicindria beck that still runs along the beguinage walls today. The beguinage was so prosperous that the citizens of Sint-Truiden were angered by its privileges and plundered it in 1340. The Wars of Religion brought about further plunderings. Much later in 1688, the people again plundered it. The rest of the beguinage was not restored until the eighteenth century. In 1796 it became state property and in 1923 the condition of the buildings was so poor that dereliction seemed inevitable. However, a group of friends was formed to get the buildings protected. Today the beguinage is a heterogeneous complex, built around a square with the church as the focal point.

Points and objects of interest

The church is a rare example of early Gothic architecture, dating from the early fourteenth century. It has several unique wall paintings, one of which is the Vera Icon, dating from around 1300. The others are art treasures from the fifteenth, sixteenth and seventeenth centuries. The 38 paintings belong to one of the most important collections in Belgium. Situated at the very back of the church is the oldest Baroque organ in Belgium. It still works. Today, the old church houses the provincial museum. A unique feature is that the beguinage farm is situated within the court walls.

Bibliography

Het begijnhof te Sint-Truiden en de oude muurschilderingen, Kunst en Oudheden in Limburg, 4 (Sint-Truiden, 1974); C. G. DEDIJN, 'Het begijnhof te Sint-Truiden en zijn nieuwe bestemming: een menselijke ontmoetingsplaats met kunst-patrimoniale en museologische objectieven', *Historische bijdragen opgedragen aan Monseigneur Dr. H. Kesters* (Sint-Truiden, 1971), pp. 49-74; M.-L. GOETHALS, *Het begijnhof van Sint-Truiden (1258-1410)* [unpublished master's dissertation Katholieke Universiteit Leuven] (Leuven, 1964); J. GRAUWELS, *Regestenlijst der oorkonden van het begijnhof te Sint-Truiden* (Brussels, 1962); *Oude kunst uit de verzameling van de 'Vrienden van het Begijnhof' te Sint-Truiden*, Kunst en Oudheden in Limburg, 3 (Sint-Truiden, 1974); F.J. STRAVEN, *Notice historique sur de béguinage dit de Sainte-Agnes à Saint-Trond* (Sint-Truiden, 1876); A. THIJS, *Het Sint-Truidens begijnhof*, Doorheen het aloude Sint-Truiden, 11 (Sint-Truiden, 1965).

| 12 | Tongeren

History

Beguines were first mentioned in Tongeren in 1243. Oda and Ida of Lude led a small community of poor women. In 1257, the authorities decided to found a full beguinage inside the city walls, alongside Geer beck. This could possibly be the oldest extant beguinage. In the centre of the beguinage stands the St. Catherine church, and an infirmary. In 1322, there were twenty-one wooden houses. Most of the present day houses are brick and date from the seventeenth century. The court consists of six streets, a gateway, a church, a graveyard, a hospital with a chapel, a brewery, three wells, a hospice and, strangely enough, a hall for festivities. At the beginning of the nineteenth century secularisation began. The infirmary became an orphanage. The St. Ursula chapel was turned into a municipal boys school. The St. Joseph convent on the other hand served as a school for girls and a home for the poor. The last beguine died in 1846 and the beguinage fell into decay. Franciscans have taken care of the church since 1899. In 1998 the town of Tongeren became responsible for the physical upkeep.

Points and objects of interest

The church dates back to 1294 and houses many valuable paintings, sculptures and religious furnishings and artefacts. Since 1999, the church has been made multipurpose: an exhibition hall, a conference centre, a concert hall...

Bibliography

H. BAILLIEN, 'Het begijnhof van Tongeren, zijn aanleg, plaatsnamen, gebouwen en bewoonsters', *Het Oude Land van Loon* 24 (1970) 61-64; *Het Catharinabegijnhof te Tongeren,* Kunst en Oudheden in Limburg, 11 (Sint-Truiden, 1975); J. HELSEN, *De rijkdom van het Tongerse Sint-Catharinabegijnhof* (Tongeren, 1999); C.M.T. THIJS, *Histoire du béguinage Ste-Cathérine à Tongres* (Tongeren, 1881); J.J.M. VAN ORMELINGEN, 'Aannemingen van begijnen in het Tongers begijnhof van 1574 tot 1673', *Het Oude Land van Loon* 31 (1977) 5-32.

| 13 | Turnhout

History

According to legend, the beguinage was founded by Mary of Brabant, Duchess of Gelder, after having a dream. Mary wanted to found a monastery, but in her dream, she had only seen beguines, so she decided to establish a beguinage. In 1372, she gave many privileges to the beguinage of Turnhout. Around 1570, the beguinage burned down and was subsequently rebuilt during the reign of the Archdukes Albert and Isabella. The new church was consecrated in 1665, when the community was at its height. In a map of 1642 the beguinage included a horse-powered mill, a barn, a pond, cropping land, and an infirmary with a farm and a meadow. During the Napoleonic period, the beguines were allowed to remain in the beguinage, but were required to pay rent. Like elsewhere, a lack of candidates in the twentieth century meant the end of the beguine community.

Points and objects of interest

The beguinage is very well preserved. The church is in typical Baroque architecture, as is its interior. The stained glass windows depict the genealogy of St. Begga. The newly-restored Beguine Museum is one of the best and biggest in Belgium. It cleverly imitates the rooms and interiors of rich beguines.

Bibliography

Het begijnhof van Turnhout. Gids voor de bezoekers, s.d.; *'t Begijntje* (periodical from the Turnhout beguinage); H. DE KOK, *Het begijnhof van Turnhout* (Turnhout, *s.d.*); IDEM, 'De eerste begijnhofkerk te Turnhout', *Archaeologica Mediaevalis* 3 (1980) 42; IDEM, 'De ingangspoort van het Turnhouts begijnhof (1700)', *Taxandria* 58 (1986) 123-125; IDEM, *Kennismaking met het Turnhouts begijnhof* (Turnhout, 1982); F. JACOBS, *Het begijnhof van Turnhout: Gids voor de bezoekers* (Turnhout, 1961); J. JANSEN, *Het kunstpatrimonium van het begijnhof te Turnhout: Foto-inventaris van het Belgische Kunstbezit. Openbare Centra voor Maatschappelijk Welzijn, Provincie Antwerpen* (Brussels and Turnhout, 1988); *Statuten en gebruiken van het begijnhof te Turnhout* (Mechelen, 1931); A.J. VAN MIERT, *Het begijnhof van Turnhout* (Turnhout, 1923); E. WAUTERS, 'De oudste "wand" van Turnhout?', *Taxandria*

56 (1984) 219-224; IDEM, 'De restauratie van het "Achterhuis" van het begijnhof te Turnhout', *Taxandria Nieuws* 18 (2000) 2:2-3; IDEM, 'Een vondst in de Turnhoutse begijnhofsite', *Taxandria* 79 (1997) 249-251.

| CONCLUSION |

We tried to provide a concise but complete summary of one of the most important spiritual movements in the history of the Lowlands. The beguine movement originated in the twelfth century. We have shown that the movement owed much to the wider social and cultural developments summarised in the phrase: "The Twelfth-Century Renaissance". The movement was part of a much wider religious renewal of the period, involving lay movements (some heretical) and sharing common elements with many other religious movements. Socio-economic changes, such as the position of women, marital status, and urbanisation, are shown to have played important roles.

In the late twelfth century many orthodox and heterodox religious movements emerged, but they existed mostly for a short time only. Members of many revivalist movements were disparagingly called 'beguines'. Among these movements, there were some spiritually-engaged groups of women who shared certain features. They were dedicated to a new form of religious life and mysticism, the *vita apostolica*. Their ideals were poverty, a dislike of ornamentation, a preference for manual labour, and works of mercy. These separate groups gradually united and moved into enclosed courts called beguinages. They were compelled to institutionalise in order to distinguish themselves from heretical movements. The establishing of beguinages thus meant the end of a revolutionary phase, necessary for survival.

Because of the enthusiasm and perseverance of the first groups the whole movement was soon recognised by the Church, be it not officially or not as a religious order, because the beguines had not taken vows. That recognition did not take place easily. The first groups were often confused with movements that would later come into conflict with the Inquisition. The beguine movement emerged in the Low Countries and expanded in the Rhineland, France, Italy, Poland, Bohemia and Silesia. Despite difficulties, they were able to protect their identity and to live in a semi-religious way up to the twentieth century when they died out. Today, romanticism prevails over reality. Beguinages are considered as model villages within towns, while beguines are thought to be pious elderly women. The beguinage of Bruges is in this respect a typical example of a tourist attraction.

We have stressed the importance of the mystical spirituality that was widely practised over many generations of beguines. Their mystical spirituality was an important feature in the history of the beguine movement, but it would also lead to its eventual downfall. We have argued that mysticism was important to beguine identity in reaction to rational scholastic theology practised by men. What has emerged is that the mysticism and the beguines' commitment to the ideal of poverty, caused conflict with the Church. After the Council of Vienne, they were forced to disappear or to be assimilated into other orders, such as the Cistercian ones.[1] This was true for most other countries, but in the Low Countries, they were able to survive, even though they never gained official ecclesiastical status.

Individual beguinages had their own organisations, statutes and regulations, acquired distinct rights, and so on. It is difficult to condense these differences and attempt to give a coherent summary of what they held in common. The entire beguine life was characterised by austerity in clothing, food and social interaction. In their daily life, priority was given to devotional exercises, taking care of the ill and frail, and manual labour. It was for this that they were known by the wider public. But during the twentieth century beguines themselves have disappeared.

1.   On the beguine parochial organisation under Cistercian auspices: MCDONNELL, *The Beguines*, pp. 170-186.

| APPENDIX |

LIST OF BEGUINAGES
IN THE FORMER LOW COUNTRIES

This list is based on P. MAJÉRUS, 'Les béguinages de Belgique: au-delà du mythe', *Bulletin de Dexia Banque* 54 (2000) 49-52; S. VAN AERSCHOT & M. HEIRMAN, *Flemish Beguinages: World Heritage* (Leuven, 2001), pp. 248-267, and W. SIMONS, *Cities of Ladies. Beguine Communities in the Medieval Low Countries (1200-1565)*, The Middle Ages Series (Philadelphia, PA, 2001), pp. 255-259. The 'oldest record' means that the beguinage was established in the year mentioned, or shortly before. The date of disappearance is often the year wherein the beguinage turned into another order or congregation, was destroyed, or the last beguine left the beguinage.

Place	Name	Oldest record	Disappearance
Aalst	St. Catherine	1261	1953
Aardenburg	St. Catherine	1249	1487-1499
Aarschot	St. Joseph & Virgin Mary	1251	1856
Aire-sur-la-Lys	?	1292	1793
Amsterdam	Virgin Mary, St. Ursula & St. John	1307	1971
Anderlecht	St. Peter & St. Guidon	1252	French period
Antwerp	Court Sion, later St. Catherine	1246	1986
Arras	10 beguinages	1246-1324	1320-1547
Assebroek	"Engelendale"	15th c.?	Shortly later
Assenede	Beguinage of "Maddijch"	1251	Mid 15th c.
Ath	Beguinage "Maillet-Boudant" or "Pont-au-Moulin"	1416	1463
Aulnoy	?	1248	1796
Avesnes	St. Mary Magdalene	1292	1748
Beaumont	Francq beguinage, St. John & Virgin Mary	1281	French period

Place	Name	Oldest record	Disappearance
Bergues	St. Elisabeth	1259	1310-1311
Béthune	?	1299	1370
Biervliet	"Rosendale"	1293	1377?
Bilzen	Virgin Mary of Seven Labour Pains or St. Barbara	1256	1860
Binche	Beguinage of Cantimpret or St. Elisabeth	1265	1598
Borgloon	Beguinage of Grathem	1258	1813
Bouvignes	Beguinage Robinoit	1420	After 1606
Braine-l'-Alleud	Beguinage of the "Motte"	1394	1528
Braine-le-Compte	St. Elisabeth	1304	1528
Breda	St. Catherine	1267	1990
Bruges	Princely beguinage "Ten Wijngaerder"	1242	1927
Brussels	Grand beguinage "Virgin Mary in the Vineyard"	1250	1844
Brussels	Small beguinage	1646	1797
Calais	2 beguinages	1335	14th c.
Cambrai	3 beguinages	1301-1354	After 1528-1529
Cantimpré	?	1233	1796
Champfleury	St. Elisabeth	1245	1477
Damme	St. Agnes	1273	1466
Deinze	St. Margareth	1273	1381-1382
Dendermonde	St. Alexis	1272	1975
Diest	St. Catherine	1245	1928
Diksmuide	St. Godeliph	1273	1914
Dinant	Beguinage of Leffe or Small hospital	1242	1466
Dinant	Beguinage of "Heillewis"	?	?
Dinant	Beguinage of Arras	1312	?
Dinant	Beguinage Alart de Brogne	1344	1466
Dinant	Beguinage Lambert le Sage	1418	1466
Dinant	Beguinage Wautier de Coraine	1458	?
Dinant	Beguinage of St. Médard	1473	?
Douai	15 beguinages	1265-1355	14th-15th c.
Duffel	Beguinage of Bethlehem	1651	1871
Eindhoven	?	1490	1567
Enghien	St. Magdalene	1255	1847
Gent	Grand Beguinage or St. Elisabeth	1233	1874
Gent	Small Beguinage or Beguinage Virgin Mary "Ter Hoye"	1262	Still 1 beguine living
Gent	"Poortakker"	1278	1798
Gent-St.-Amandsberg	St.-Elisabeth	1874	Still 1 beguine living
Geraardsbergen	St. Margareth	1247	1846
Grave	?	1394	1659
Grez-Doiceau	Beguinage of Péry	13th c.	French period
Halen	?	1526	?
Halle	?	1412	?
Hasselt	St. Catherine	1245	1857
Helmond	?	1426	1693
Hénin-Liétard	?	1282	1693
Herentals	Virgin Mary & St. Catherine	1266	1997
's-Hertogenbosch	Grand Beguinage, Virgin Mary	1274	1675
's-Hertogenbosch	Small Beguinage	1349	1591
Hesdin	?	1248	1345
Hocht	?	1267	After 1267
Hoogstraten	St. John the Baptist	1381	1972
Hulst	St. Agnes	1295	1458

Place	Name	Oldest record	Disappearance
Huy	28 beguine houses	1251	French period
Ieper	Beguinage of Brielen or St. Christina	1240	1842
Ieper	Beguinage of Baerdonck or St. Thomas	1273	1422
Ieper	Black Beguinage	?	1422
IJzendijke	?	1276	1404?
Jodoigne	?	1382	18th c.
Kortrijk	St. Elisabeth	1240	Still 1 beguine living
Lens-Saint-Remy	St. Mary Magdalene	1243	Beginning 14th c.
Le Quesnoy	?	1246	1462
Lessines	?	?	Beginning 15th c.
Leuven	Grand Beguinage "Ten Hove", St. John the Baptist	1232	1988
Leuven	Small Beguinage	1295	1855
Liège	St. Christopher	1224	Mid 19th c.
Liège	Several other (maybe 78) beguinages		Last one: 1890
Lier	St. Margareth	1258	1994
Lille	St. Elisabeth	1244-1245	1855
Maaseik	St. Agnes	1265	1482
Maastricht	St. Catherine	1251	1502
Maastricht	St. Andrew	1264	1426
Maldegem	?	1343	End 15th c.
Malèves (Perwez)	?	1267	?
Marck	?	1302	After 1320
Masnuy	?	1273	?
Maubeuge	?	1267	1679
Mechelen	Grand Beguinage or St. Catherine & St. Alexis	1259	1993
Mechelen	Small Beguinage or St. Mary Magdalene	1245	1822
Mesen	?	Before 1300?	1553
Momalle	Beguinage Nicolas Quartael	1366	French period
Mons	Beguinage de Cantimpret	1245	French period
Mons	Beguinage of Mons or St. Germain	End 13th c.	14th c.
Mont-Saint-Éloi	?	1312	After 1312
Morlanwelz	?	1572	French period
Namur	Grand Beguinage "Hors-Postil" or St. Aubain	1235	1650
Namur	St. Symphorian	1279	1467
Namur	Beguinage du Coq	Beginning 14th c. ?	1498
Namur	Beguinage Delle Tour	1269	Beginning 15th c.
Namur	Beguinage of Rhyne	1420	1568
Namur	Beguinage Dupont	1398	Shortly later
Namur	Beguinage of the Four Daughters in Cuvirue	1593	French period
Nieuwpoort	St. John	1314	Before 1914
Ninove	?	1370	1475
Nivelles	St. Sepulchre	1282	15th c.
Nivelles	Beguinage of Goutisseau Gouthal	1272	17th c.
Nivelles	Beguinage of Willambroux	1282	17th c.
Nivelles	Beguinage of the "Royauté"	1272	16th c.
Nivelles	Beguinage Duquette	1468	1713
Nivelles	Small Beguinage or Beguinage "de la Tourelle"	1713	1836

Place	Name	Oldest record	Disappearance
Noirhat	?	1267	Before the 15th c.
Oignies	?	1239	1352
Oisterwijk	Bethlehem	1559	1725
Oostburg	?	1269	1550-1551
Orchies	?	1273	1538
Oudenaarde	St. Roch	1367	1960
Oudenaarde	Court of Sion	Beginning 15th c.	15th c.
Oudenaarde	Beguinage of Pamele	1409	16th c.
Oud-Heusden	?	1390	Late 16th c.
Overijse	Beguinage "Mariëndal"	1267	French period
Perwez	?	1325	?
Roermond	St. Catherine	1279	1797
Ronse	?	1394	1602
Saint-Omer	21 convents	1307-1317	1327-16th c.
Sin	?	1309	1587
Sint-Truiden	St. Agnes	c. 1258	1860
Sittard	?	1276	1677
Soignies	St. James	c. 1260	1489
Temse	?	1566	?
Thorembais-les-Béguines?		1256	French period
Thorn	?	1287	1797
Thuin	St. Elisabeth	1558	Shortly later
Tielt	?	Beginning 14th c.	1393
Tienen	St. Agatha, later Virgin Mary	1250	1857
Tongeren	St. Catherine	1243	1856
Torhout	?	1275	1501
Tournai	Beguinage of Magdalene of the Fields	1241	1846
Tournai	Beguinage "As Degrés"	1251	15th c.
Tournai	St. Catherine	?	?
Turnhout	St. Catherine	1340	1998
Valenciennes	St. Elisabeth	1239	1796
Veurne	?	1273	1511
Vilvoorde	Virgin Mary	1239	1840
Walcourt	?	1239	?
Wavre	?	End 13th c.	16th c.
Ways (Nivelles)	?	1545	?
Wetz	Holy Spirit	1245	1752
Yves	?	1239	?
Zichem	Beguinage "Elzenklooster"	1438	15th c.
Zoutleeuw	Beguinage of Griecken	1245	French period

| BIBLIOGRAPHY |

General Bibliography for the Study of Beguines and Beguinages (with particular attention to the Low Countries and to English, German and French publications)

An older but very extended bibliography can be found in L.J. M. PHILIPPEN, *De begijnhoven: oorsprong, geschiedenis, inrichting* (Antwerp, 1918), pp. 435-472 and in A.MENS, *Oorsprong en betekenis van de Nederlandse begijnen-en begardenbeweging: vergelijkende studie (XIIde-XIIIde eeuw)* (Antwerp, 1947), pp. xi-xxx. More recent bibliography: MAJÉRUS, P. *Ces femmes qu'on dit béguines... Guide des béguinages de Belgique. Bibliographie et sources d'archives*, Introduction bibliographique à l'histoire des couvents belges antérieure à 1796, 9 (Brussels, 1997).

ASEN, J., 'Die Beginen in Köln', *Annalen des historischen Vereins für den Niederrhein insbesondere die alte Erzdiözese Köln* 111 (1927) 81-180; 112 (1928) 71-148; 113 (1928) 13-96.

AXTERS, S., *Geschiedenis van de vroomheid in de Nederlanden*, 4 vols. (Antwerp, 1950-1960).

Begijnhoven in de provincie Limburg, Kunst en Oudheden in Limburg, 4 (Sint-Truiden, 1974).

BERNARTS, M., *Speculum Virginum: Geistigkeit und Seelenleben der Frau im Hochmittelalter*, Beihefte zum Archiv für Kulturgeschichte, 16 (Cologne/Vienna, 1982).

BERTIN, P., 'Le béguinage d'Aire-Sur-La-Lys (13ᵉ-17ᵉ s.)', *Revue du Nord* 40 (1949) 92-104.

BETERAMS, F., 'De armenzorg in het Ancien Régime en de 19ᵈᵉ eeuw', *Handelingen van de Zuidnederlandse Maatschappij voor Taal en Letterkunde en Geschiedenis* 11 (1957) 3-10.

'De BOGGAARDEN Schole', *Rond den Heerd* 5 (1870) 4.

BOGIN, M., *The Women Troubadours* (London, 1976).

BOLTON, B.M., 'Mulieres Sanctae', BROWN, D. (ed.), *Sanctity and Secularity: The Church and the World*, Studies in Church History, 10 (Oxford, 1973), pp. 77-95.

ID., 'Some Thirteenth Century Women in the Low Countries: A Special Case?', *Nederlands Archief voor Kerkgeschiedenis* 61 (1981) 7-29.

ID., 'Vitae Matrum: A Further Aspect of the "Frauenfrage"', BAKER, D. (ed.), *Medieval Women* (Oxford, 1978), pp. 253-273.

BONENFANT, P., *Hôpitaux et bienfaisance publique dans les anciens Pays-Bas des origines à la fin du 18ᵉ siècle. I: Les hôpitaux en Belgique au Moyen Âge,* Annales de la Société Belge d'Histoire des Hôpitaux, 3 (Brussels, 1965).

BYNUM, C.W., *Holy Feast and Holy Fast: The Religious Significance of Food to Medieval Women* (Berkeley, CA, 1987).

ID., 'Women Mystics and Eucharistic Devotion in the Thirteenth Century', *Women's Studies* 11 (1984) 179-214.

CALLAY, F., 'De Beggaerden in de Nederlanden, tijdens de Middeleeuwen', *Handelingen van de Vlaamse Filologencongressen* 2 (1913) 4.

CAMBIER, A., 'Het begijnhof te Ronse', *Annalen van de Geschied- en Oudheidkundige Kring van Ronse en het tenement Inde* 11 (1962) 41-45, 47-52, 56-88; 12 (1963) 78-80; 13 (1964) 130-178; 14 (1965) 59-67, 119-127; 15 (1966) 153-183; 16 (1967) 57-70.

CARPENTIER, B., *Le Béguinage Sainte Elisabeth de Valenciennes de sa fondation au 16ᵉ siècle* (Valenciennes, 1959).

CELIS, G., 'De begijnhoven in Oost-Vlaanderen: geschiedkundige studie', *Oostvlaamsche Zanten* 4 (1929) 88-94.

CEYSSENS, L., 'Eenige oorkonden over het begijnhof te Aardenburg', *Handelingen van het Genootschap voor Geschiedenis Société d'Emulation te Brugge* 1-2 (1935) 59-102.

CLEMENT, T., GHOBERT, J. & HUART, C., *Les anciennes constructions rurales et les petites constructions des béguinages en Belgique*, 3 vols. (Brussels, 1914-1917).

COGEN-LEDEGANCK, C., *Begijntjes en Begijnhoven* (Antwerp, 1901).

CONN, M.A., *Noble Daoughters: Unheralded Women in Western Christianity, 13th to 18th Centuries*, Contributions to the Study of Religion, 60 (Westport, CT., 2000), pp. 1-26.

DE BADTS, H.A., 'Brieven', *Rond den Heerd* 3 (1868) 319-320.

DEBLAERE, A., 'Preghiera: VI. La preghiera tra le beghine e nella *devotio moderna*', *Dizionario degli Istituti di Perfezione* 7 (1983) 655-666.

DEGLER-SPENGLER, B., 'Die religiöse Frauenbewegung des Mittelalters: Konversen, Nonnen, Beginen', *Rottenburger Jahrbuch für Kirchengeschichte* 3 (1984) 75-88.

DE KEYZER, W., 'Aspects de la vie béguinale à Mons aux 13e et 14e siècles', *Autour de la ville en Hainaut. Mélanges d'archéologie et d'histoire urbaines offerts à J.Dugnoille et à Sansen*, Études et documents du Cercle Royal d'Histoire et d'Archéologie d'Ath et de la Région et Musées Athois, 7 (Ath, 1986), pp. 205-226.

DELMAIRE, B., 'Les béguines dans le Nord de la France au premier siècle de leur histoire (vers 1230-vers 1350)', PARISSE, M. (ed.), *Les religieuses en France au 13e siècle* (Nancy, 1985) pp. 121-162.

DELMELLE, J., *Enkele abdijen en begijnhoven van België*, Teksten en Documenten. Verzameling 'Belgische Kroniek', 294 (Brussels, 1973).

DENSLAGEN, W.F., 'Begijnhoven in Noord-Nederlandse steden', *Bulletin van de Koninklijke Nederlandse Oudheidkundige Bond* 77 (1978) 205-224.

DEROLEZ, A., 'A Devotee of Saint Barbara in a Belgian Beguinage (Marston Ms.287)', *Yale University Library Gazette Supplement*, 66 (New Haven, CT, 1991).

DESCHAMPS, J., 'De Herkomst van het Leidse handschrift van Sint-Servatiuslegende van Hendrik van Veldeke', *Handelingen van de Zuidnederlandse Maatschappij voor Taal en Letterkunde en Geschiedenis* 12 (1958) 53-78.

DEVLIN, D., *Feminine Lay Piety in the High Middle Ages: The Beguines*, NICHOLS J.A. & SHANK, L.T. (eds.), *Distant Echoes: Medieval Religious Women*, Cistercian Studies Series, 71 (Kalamazoo, 1984), pp.183-196.

DE VROEDE, M., *Religieuses et béguines enseignantes dans les Pays-Bas Méridionaux et la Principauté de Liège aux 17ᵉ-18ᵉ siècles*, Studia Paedagogica, 20 (Leuven, 1996).

D'HAENENS, A. (ed.), *Begijnhoven van België* (Brussels, 1979).

ID., 'Femmes excédentaires et vocation religieuse dans l'ancien diocèse de Liège lors de l'essor urbain (fin du 12ᵉ-début du 13ᵉ siècle): le cas d'Ide de Nivelles (1200-1231)', *Hommage à la Wallonie. Mélanges offerts à M.-A. Arnould et P. Ruelle* (Brussels, 1981), pp. 217-235.

DINZELBACHER, P. & BAUER, D.R., *Religiöse Frauenbewegung und mystische Frömmigkeit im Mittelalter*, Beihefte zum Archiv für Kulturgeschichte, 28 (Cologne, 1988).

DOR, J. et al., *New Trends in Feminine Spirituality. The Holy Women of Liège and their Impact* (Turnhout, 1999).

DRONKE, P., *Women Writers of the Middle Ages: A Critical Study of Texts from Perpetua to Marguerite Porete* (New York, 1984).

DUVERNOY, J., *Cathares, Vaudois et béguins: dissidents du pays d'Oc*, Collection Domaine cathare (Toulouse, 1994).

'Een EIGENAARDIG Begijntjes-Lofdicht', *Oostvlaamsche Zanten* 4 (1929) 95-97.

F. Elias van Sinte Teresa, *Het Gheestelyck Palays der Beggynhoven in dry boecken verdeylt (...)* (Antwerp, 1926).

Elm, K., 'Beg(h)arden', *Lexikon des Mittelalters* (Munich, 1980), vol. 1, col. 1798.

Id., Sprendel, R. & Manselli, R., 'Beg(h)inen', *Lexikon des Mittelalters* (Munich, 1980), vol. 1, col. 1799-1803.

Epiney-Burgard, G., 'L'influence des béguines sur Ruusbroec', Mommaers, P. & De Paepe, N. (eds.), *Jan van Ruusbroec* (Leuven, 1984).

Id., & Zum Brunn, E., *Femmes Troubadours de Dieu* (Turnhout, 1988).

Faesen, R., *Lichaam in lichaam, ziel in ziel: Christusbeleving bij Hadewijch en haar tijdgenoten* (Baarn and Gent, 2003).

Fraeters, V., 'Hadewijch', Aercke, K. (ed.), *Women Writing in Dutch* (New York, 1994).

Freed, J. B., 'Urban Development and the "Cura Monialium" in Thirteenth-Century Germany', *Viator* 3 (1972) 311-327.

Gies, F. & J., *Women in the Middle Ages* (New York, 1980).

Gijsen, J., *Vlaamse begijnhoven ontdekken en beleven. Een sfeervolle zoektocht naar een heel eigen verleden* (Aartselaar, 1999).

Goossens, J., 'Gebeeldhouwde piëta's en laatmiddeleeuwse begijnen in de Zuidelijke Nederlanden: een nieuwe relatie', *Handelingen der Maatschappij voor Geschiedenis en Oudheidkunde te Gent* 75 (1992) 239-245.

Id., *De kwestie Lambertus 'li Beges' († 1177)*, Verhandelingen van de Koninklijke Academie voor Wetenschappen, Letteren en Schone Kunsten van België, 110 (Brussels, 1984).

Greven, J., *Die Anfänge der Beginen. Ein Beitrag zur Geschichte der Volksfrömmigkeit und des Ordenswesens im Hochmittelalter*, Vorreformationsgeschichtliche Forschungen, 8 (Münster, 1912).

Id., 'Der Ursprung des Beginenwesens: eine Auseinandersetzung mit Godefroid Kurth', *Historisches Jahrbuch* 35 (1914) 46-47.

GROTE, G., *De Semonia ad Beghinas*, ed. DE VREESE ('s Gravenhage, 1940).

GRUNDMANN, H., 'Zur Geschichte der Beginen im 13. Jahrhundert', *Archiv für Kulturgeschichte* 21 (1931) 296-320.

ID., *Religiöse Bewegungen im Mittelalter. Untersuchungen über die geschichtlichen Zusammenhänge zwischen der Ketzerei, den Betelorden und der religiösen Frauenbewegung im 12. und 13. Jahrhundert und über die geschichtlichen Grundlagen der deutschen Mystik*, Historische Studien, 267 (Berlin, 1935 and 1961²).

HAESAERTS, P., 'Onze Begijnhoven. Eenige aantekeningen over hunne geschiedenis in 't algemeen', *Vlaamsch Leven* 2 (1916) 117-120.

ID., 'Onze Vlaamsche Begijnen. Enige Wetenswaardigheden over haar leven en regel', *Vlaamsch Leven* 2 (1917) 436-442.

HALIN, J., *Begijnhoven* (Brussels, 1943).

HALLMANN, E., *Geschichte des Ursprungs der Belgischen Beghinen* (Berlin, 1843).

HEIRMAN, M., *Langs Vlaamse begijnhoven*, Leuven, 2001.

ID. & BUYLE, M., 'Een vernieuwd begijnhofmuseum', *Monumenten en Landschappen* 19 (2000) 3:45-63.

HELVÉTIUS, J.-M., 'Les béguines: des femmes dans la ville aux 13e et 14e siècles', GUBIN, E. & NANDRIN, J.-P. (ed.), *La ville et les femmes en Belgique: histoire et sociologie*, Travaux et Recherches, 18 (Brussels, 1993), pp. 17-40.

HILKA, A., 'Altfranzösische Mystik und Beginentum', *Zeitschrift für romanische Philologie* 47 (1927) 121-170.

HOORNAERT, H., *Ce que c'est qu'un Béguinage* (Lille, 1921).

HUYGENS, R.B.C., *Lettres de Jacques de Vitry* (Leiden, 1960).

JANSSEN, H.Q., 'Oorkonde betrekkelijk de hervorming van het Aardenburgse begijnhof in een klooster van de derde Orde van de H. Franciscus (1499)', *Bijdragen tot de Oudheidkunde en de Geschiedkunde inzonderheid van Zeeuwsch-Vlaanderen* (1856), 323-326.

JUTEN, G.C.A., 'Kloosters en gestichten, allen verdwenen. Begijnhof', *Bulletin uitgegeven door den Nederlandschen Oudheidkundigen Bond* (1924) 207.

KING, M. (ed.), *The Life of Marie d'Oignies*, Peregrina Translations Series (Saskatoon, 1986).

KING, M.H., 'The Desert Mothers Revisited. The Mothers of the Diocese of Liège', *Vox Benedictina* 5 (1988) 325-354.

KOCH, E., *Frauenfrage und Ketzertum im Mittelalter: die Frauenbewegung im Rahmen des Katharismus und des Waldensertums und ihre sozialen Wurzeln (12.-14.Jahrhundert)*, Forschungen zur mittelalterlichen Geschichte, 9 (Berlin, 1962).

ID., 'Kloosterintrede, huwelijk en familiefortuin. De kosten van klooster en huwelijk voor adellijke vrouwen in zuidoost-Nederland in de late middeleeuwen', *In de schaduw van de eeuwigheid. Tien studies over religie en samenleving in laatmiddeleeuws Nederland aangeboden aan Prof. dr. A.H. Bredero* (Utrecht, 1986), pp. 242-257.

ID., 'De positie van vrouwen op de huwelijksmarkt in de Middeleeuwen', *Tijdschrift voor Sociale Geschiedenis* 13 (1987) 150-172.

KOORN, F., 'Women Without Vows: The Case of the Beguines and the Sisters of the Common Life in the Northern Netherlands', SCHULTE VAN KESSEL, E. (ed.), *Women and Men in Spiritual Culture: XIV-XVII Centuries* ('s-Gravenhage, 1984), 135-147.

KOORN, F.W.J., *Begijnhoven in Holland en Zeeland gedurende de middeleeuwen* (Assen, 1981).

ID., 'Ongebonden vrouwen: overeenkomsten en verschillen tussen begijnen en zusters van het Gemene Leven', *Ons Geestelijk Erf* 58 (1985) 393-402.

ID. & VAN DER EYCKEN, M., *Begijnen in Brabant* ('s-Gravenhage, 1987).

KOWALCZEWSKI, J., 'Thirteenth Century Asceticism: Marie d'Oignies and Lutgard of Aywières as Active and Passive

Ascetics. With Extracts from Their Vitae Selected and Translated by M.H. King', *Vox Benedictina* 3 (1986) 20-50.

KURTH, G., 'Origine liégeoise des Béguines', *Bulletin de l'Académie royale de Belgique, Classe des lettres* (1912) 437-462.

KURTZ, D., 'Mary of Oignies, Christine the Marvelous, and Medieval Heresy', *Mystics Quarterly* 14 (1988) 186-196.

LAUWERS, J., *Peutie en zijn voormalig begijnhof van Steenvoort* (Tielt, 1976).

LAUWERS, M., 'Expérience béguinale et récit hagiographique. À propos de la 'Vita Mariae Oigniacensis' de Jacques de Vitry (vers 1215)', *Journal des Savants* (1989) 61-103.

ID., 'Paroles de femmes, sainteté féminine: l'Église du 13e siècle face aux béguines', BRAIVE, G. & CAUCHIES, J.-M. (eds.), *La critique historique à l'épreuve. Liber discipulorum Jacques Paquet* (Brussels, 1989), pp. 99-115.

LE BRAS, G., 'Institutions ecclésiastiques de la Chrétienté médiévale', FLICHE, A. & MARTIN, V., *Histoire de l'église* (Paris, 1959), vol. 12, pp. 171-178.

LECOUTERE, C., 'Eene legende over den oorsprong der Begijnen', *Koninklijke Vlaamse Academie voor Taal en Letterkunde. Verslagen en mededelingen* (1907) 96-134.

LERNER, R.E., 'Beguines and Beghards', STRAYER, J. (ed.), *Dictionary of the Middle Ages* (New York), vol. 2, pp. 157-162.

Het LEVEN van de seer edele, doorluchtighste en H. Begga Hertoginne van Brabant, stighteresse der Beggijnen, met een cort begrijp van de Levens der Salige, Godtvruchtighe en Lof-weerdige beggyntjens der vermaerde en hoogh-gepresen Beggijnhoven, bij een vergadert door eenen onbekenden Dienaer Godts (Antwerp, 1712).

LINDEMANS, J., 'Uit oude papieren. Vilvoorde: eene bisschoppelijke vermaning aan de begijnen', *Eigen Schoon en De Brabander* 17 (1934) 17-18.

LITTLE, L.K., *Religious Poverty and the Profit Economy in*

Medieval Europe (London, 1978).

LORIE, A., 'Le Béguinage d'Overyssche', *Folklore Brabançon* 3 (1923-4) 105-106.

M., 'Brieven', *Rond den Heerd* 3 (1868) 310-311.

MAES, P., 'Les béguinages', *Trésors des béguinages* (Gent, 1961).

MAJÉRUS, P., *Ces femmes qu'on dit béguines... Guide des béguinages de Belgique. Bibliographie et sources d'archives*, Introduction bibliographique à l'histoire des couvents belges antérieure à 1796, 9 (Brussels, 1997).

ID., 'De begijnhoven in België: mythe en werkelijkheid', *Het Tijdschrift van Dexia Bank* 54 (2000) 33-53 [French version: 'Les béguinages de Belgique: au-delà du mythe', *Bulletin de Dexia Banque* 54 (2000) 33-53]

MCDONNELL, E.W., *The Beguines and Beghards in Medieval Culture. With Special Emphasis on the Belgian Scene* (New Brunswick, NJ, 1954).

MCNAMARA, J.A.K., 'De Quibusdam Mulieribus: Reading Women's History from Hostile Sources', ROSENTHAL, J.T. (ed.), *Medieval Women and the Sources of Medieval History* (Athens, GA, 1990).

MENS, A., *Beghini, begardi, beghinaggi, Dizionario degli Istituti di Perfezione*, I, Rome, 1974 col.1165-1180.

ID., 'Les béguines et les béghards dans le cadre de la culture médiévale', *Le Moyen Age* 64 (1958) 305-315.

ID., *Nederlandse begijnen- en begardenbeweging* (Antwerp, 1944).

ID., *Oorspong en betekenis van de Nederlandse begijnen- en begardenbeweging. Vergelijkende studie: XII^{de}-XIII^{de} eeuw* (Antwerp, 1947).

ID., 'De vereering van de H.Eucharistie bij onze vroegste begijnen', *Studia eucharistica DCC anni a condito festo sanctissimi Corporis Christi (1246-1946)* (Antwerp, 1946).

MERTENS, T. (ed.), 'Vrouwen en mystiek in de Nederlanden', *Ons Geestelijk Erf* 65 (1992) 1-144.

MILIS, L., 'Het begijnenwezen: uiting van een middeleeuwse maatschappij in de kering', *Toespraken gehouden bij de begijnhoffeesten, Breda, juni 1980* (Breda, 1980), pp. 9-29.

MOMMAERS, P., *Hadewijch: Writer, Beguine, Love Mystic* (Leuven, 2004).

MONNON, P., *Les mulieres sanctae de l'ancien diocèse de Liège et leurs hagiographes masculins. Un propos de Vita Sancta au 13ᵉ siècle* (Brussels, 1992).

MONTEIRO, M., *Geestelijke maagden: leven tussen klooster en wereld in Noord-Nederland gedurende de zeventiende eeuw* (Hilversum, 1996).

MULLER, D., 'Les béguines', *Actes de la deuxième session d'Histoire médiévale de Carcassone (28 août – 1ᵉʳ septembre 1989) = Hérésis* nr. 13-14.

MULLER, E., 'Heilige maagden : de verering van maagdheiligen in religieuze vrouwengemeenschappen', BANGE, P. & MULLER, E. (eds.), *Tussen heks en heilige: het vrouwbeeld op de drempel van de moderne tijd (15ᵈᵉ-16ᵈᵉ eeuw)* (Nijmegen, 1985), pp. 83-100.

MURK-JANSEN, S., *Brides in the Desert: The Spirituality of the Beguines*, Traditions of Christian Spirituality Series (Maryknoll, NY, 1998).

NEAL, C., 'The Origin of the Beguines', BENNETT, J.M., CLARK E.A., O'BARR J.F. & WESTPHAL-WIHL, S. (eds.), *Sisters and Workers in the Middle Ages* (Chicago,IL, 1989), pp. 241-260.

NEUMANN, E.G., *Rheinisches Beginen- und Begardenwesen: ein Mainzer Beitrag zur religiösen Bewegung am Rhein* (Meisenheim am Glan, 1960).

NIMAL, H., *Les Béguinages* (Nivelles, 1908).

NOLET, W. & BOEREN, P.C., *Kerkelijke instellingen in de middeleeuwen* (Amsterdam, 1951).

NÜBEL, O., *Mittelalterliche Beginen- und Sozialsiedlungen in den Niederlanden: ein Beitrag zur Vorgeschichte der Fuggerei* (Tübingen, 1970).

OLIVER, J.H., 'Begijnenspiritualiteit en boekenproductie in het oude bisdom Luik', *In beeld geprezen: Miniaturen uit Maaslandse devotieboeken (1250-1350)* (Sint-Truiden and Leuven, 1989), pp. 32-52.

ID., 'Devotional Psalters and the Study of Beguine Spirituality', *Vox Benedictina* 9 (1992) 198-225.

ID., 'The Mendicants, Lambert le Bègue, and the Beguines', SMEYERS, M. (ed.), *Gothic Manuscript Illumination in the Diocese of Liège (c. 1250-c. 1330)* Corpus of Illuminated Manuscripts in the Low Coutries, 2 (Leuven, 1988, pp. 101-122.

ID., '"Je pècheresse renc grasces a vos": Some French devotional texts in Beguine psalters', *Litterae Textuales. Medieval Codicology* (Festschrift K.V. Sinclear) (Leiden, 1994), pp. 248-266.

OPERATIE abdijen en begijnhoven in België, 2 vols. (Brussels, 1973).

OPITZ, C., 'Contraintes et libertés (1250-1500)', DUBY, G. & PERROT, M., *Histoire des femmes en Occident, t. 2: Le Moyen Age* (Paris, 1991), pp. 277-335.

'Het OUDE begijnhof van Roermond', *De Nieuwe Koerier* 20 August, 3 and 19 September 1938.

OVERVOORDE, J.C., *De rechtstoestand van de huisjes der begijnen op de begijnhoven*, Verslagen en mededelingen van de Vereniging tot de uitgave der bronnen van het oude vaderlandse recht, 2 ('s-Gravenhage, 1982), pp. 550-620.

PAQUET, J., 'Het eerste statuut der Begijnhoven opgesteld door Jacques de Troyes en uitgevaardigd door Robert de Thourotte rond 1246', *Verzamelde Opstellen* 11 (1935) 185-204.

PARISSE, M. (ed.), *Les Religieuses en France au 13e siècle. Table ronde organisée par l'Institut d'Études Médiévales à Nancy II, 25-26 juin 1983* (Nancy, 1989).

PETERS, G., 'Norddeutsches Beginen- und Begardenwesen in Mittelalter', *Niedersächsisches Jahrbuch für Landesgeschichte* 41-2 (1969-70) 50-118.

PETERS, M., 'Beguine Women: Medieval Spirituality, Modern Implications', *Review for Religious* March-April (1995) 236-244.

PETERS, U., *Religiöse Erfahrung als literarisches Faktum. Zur Vorgeschichte und Genese frauenmystischer Texte des 13. und 14. Jahrhunderts*, Hermaea. Germanistische Forschungen N.F., 56 (Tübingen, 1988).

PHILIPPEN, L.J.M., 'De begijnhoven: hunne geschiedenis', *Maandelijksch Bulletijn der Vereniging tot het Behoud van Natuur- en Stedenschoon* 8 (1929) 50-59.

ID., 'Begijnhoven en spiritualiteit', *Ons Geestelijk Erf* 3 (1929) 165-195.

ID., *De begijnhoven: oorsprong, geschiedenis, inrichting* (Antwerp, 1918).

ID., *Onze begijntjes: hun naam, hun leven* (Antwerp, 1944).

ID., LEURS, S. & VAN MIERLO, J., *De begijnhoven*, Steden en Landschappen, 7 (Antwerp, 1931).

PHILIPS, D., *Beguines in Medieval Strasburg: A Study of the Social Aspects of Beguine Life* (Palo Alto, 1941).

PRIMS, F., 'De oorsprong der Antwerpsche Beggaarden', *Antwerpiensia* 3 (1929) 23-31.

PUTEANUS, E., *De Begginarum apud Belgas instituto et nomine suffragium; quo controversia recens excitata sopitur* (Leuven, 1630).

QUINTYN, R.-M., *Normen en normering van het begijnenleven. Vergelijkende studie van de begijnenregels in de Nederlanden van de 17de tot de 18de eeuw* [unpublished master's dissertation Rijksuniversiteit Gent] (Gent, 1984).

ROBYNS, O., 'Stichting der begijnen', *Limburg* 8 (1926-7) 126-127.

ROISIN, S., 'L'efflorescence cistercienne et le courant féminin de piété au 13e siècle', *Revue d'Histoire Ecclésiastique* 39 (1943) 342-378.

Roose-Meier, B., *Begijnhof en begijnhofmuseum. Foto-inventaris van het Belgisch Kunstbezit. Openbare Centra voor Maatschappelijk Welzijn. Provincie West-Vlaanderen* (Brussels, 1990).

Ruh, K., 'Beginenmystik: Hadewijch, Mechtild von Magdeburg, Marguerite Porete', *Zeitschrift für deutsche Literatur* 106 (1977) 265-277.

Rutgeerts, A., 'Begijnen in Vlaanderen', *Volk aan den Arbeid* 2 (1943) 10.

Sabbe, M., 'Een begijnenliederboekje uit de 18de eeuw', *Volkskunde* 17 (1905) 225-231.

Schirmer, E., *Mystik und Minne. Frauen im Mittelalter,* Elefanten Press, 116 (Berlin, 1984).

Schmitt, J.-C., *Mort d'une hérésie: l'Église et les clercs face aux béguines et aux béghards du Rhin supérieur du 14e au 15e siècle*, Civilisations et sociétés, 56 (Paris, 1978).

Schuermans, L.W., 'De Fratricellen en Beggaerden', *Lettervruchten van Taal- en Letterlievend Studentengenootschap der Katholieke Hogeschool van Leuven* (1863) 123-157.

Simons, W., 'The Beguine Movement in the Southern Low Countries: A Reassessment', *Bulletin de l'Institut Historique Belge de Rome* 59 (1989) 63-105.

Id., 'Beguines and Psalters', *Ons Geestelijk Erf* 64 (1991) 23-30.

Id., 'Een zeker bestaan: de Zuidnederlandse begijnen en de Frauenfrage', *Tijdschrift voor Sociale Geschiedenis* 17 (1991) 125-146.

Sivré, J.B., 'Geschiedkundige schets van het oud begijnhof te Roermond', *Publications de la Société Historique et Archéologique dans le duché de Limbourg* 11 (1874).

Smolders, P., 'Gewoonterecht betreffende het bouwen en bewonen der begijnenhuizen in de begijnhoven', *Verzamelde Opstellen* 18 (1943) 243-256.

Staeltjen van het Leven van de H.Begga, Hertoginne van Brabandt, Fondatresse van de Begijn-hoven, Voorghesteldt

*op den Jubilé van Duysent Jaren van haeren sterfdagh.
Door M.H. Begghijntjen* (Antwerp, 1698?).

'De TENTOONSTELLING der begijnhoven', *Oostvlaamsche
Zanten* 4 (1929) 81-87.

THION, A., 'Les religieuses en Belgique du 18ᵉ au 20ᵉ siècle.
Approche statistique', *Belgisch Tijdschrift voor Nieuwste
Geschiedenis* 7 (1976) 1-55.

TISSEGHEM, R. & DAEMEN, J., *Begijnhoven vroeger en nu: 'neer-
stigh tot eere Godts'* (Groot-Bijgaarden, 1995).

TOMSIN, N., *Béguines et béguinages liègeois. Une réalité mécon-
nue et oubliée* (Liège, 1984).

TRIEST, M., *Het besloten hof: begijnen in de Zuidelijke
Nederlanden* (Leuven, 1998).

UITZ, E., *Die Frau in der Mittelalterlichen Stadt* (Freiburg-
am-Breisgau, 1992²).

VAN AERSCHOT, S. & HEIRMAN, M., *Vlaamse begijnhoven.
Werelderfgoed* (Leuven, 2001) [English version: *Flemish
Beguinages. World Heritage*]

VAN BAEST, M., 'Mystieke vrouwenbewegingen in de 13ᵈᵉ
eeuw', BAERS, J., BRINKMAN, G., JELSMA, A. & STEGGINK, O.
(eds.), *Encyclopedie van de mystiek: fundamenten, tradities
en perspectieven*, (Kampen and Tielt, 2003), pp. 684-698.

VAN BEVER, G., *Les béguinages* (Brussels, 1943).

VAN BUYTEN, L., 'Begijnen en begijnhoven', *Spiegel Historiael*
13 (1973) 532-541.

VANDENBROECK, P. (ed.), *Hooglied: de beeldwereld van
religieuze vrouwen in de Zuidelijke Nederlanden, vanaf
de dertiende eeuw* (Gent, 1994).

VAN DER HALLEN, E., 'De stervende Begijnhoven',
*Maandelijksch Bulletijn der Vereniging tot het Behoud van
Natuur- en Stedenschoon* 8 (1929) 64-66.

VANDER VELPEN, J., 'Een middeleeuws klooster op Blotenberg
bij Meldert-Hoegaarden. E: een begijnhoftraditie', *Eigen
Schoon en De Brabander* 41 (1958) 38.

Van Mechelen, J., *Avonden in het Begijnhof* (Gent, 1972).

Id., *Vlaamse begijnhoven: in schemelheyt der maechtlyckheydt* (Brussels?, 1973).

Van Mierlo, J., 'Het begardisme. Een synthetische studie', *Koninklijke Vlaamse Academie voor Taal en Letterkunde. Verslagen en mededelingen* (1930) 277-305.

Id., 'De bijnaam van Lambertus li Beges en de vroegste betekenis van het woord begijn', *Koninklijke Vlaamse Academie voor Taal en Letterkunde. Verslagen en mededelingen* (1925) 405-447.

Id., 'Les Béguines et Lambert li Beges: mise au point', *Revue d'Histoire Ecclésiastique* 23 (1927) 785-801.

Id., 'Lambert li Beges in verband met den oorsprong der begijnenbeweging', *Koninklijke Vlaamse Academie voor Taal en Letterkunde. Verslagen en mededelingen* (1926) 612-660.

Id., 'Losse beschouwingen over het ontstaan der begijnen- en begardenbeweging', *Ons Geestelijk Erf* 23 (1949) 121-149 and 247-267.

Id., 'Het ontstaan der Begijnen', *Streven* 3 (1933-4) 15-22.

Id., 'Ophelderingen bij de vroegste geschiedenis van het woord begijn', *Koninklijke Vlaamse Academie voor Taal en Letterkunde. Verslagen en mededelingen* (1931) 983-1006.

Id., 'De wederwaardigheden van een etymologie. De vroegste geschiedenis van het woord: "begijn"', *Koninklijke Vlaamse Academie voor Taal en Letterkunde. Verslagen en mededelingen* (1945) 31-51.

Vauchez, A., *Les laïcs au Moyen Âge: pratiques et expériences religieuses* (Paris, 1987).

Id., 'Prosélytisme et action antihérétique en milieu féminin au 13e siècle : La Vie de Marie d'Oignies (†1213) par Jacques De Vitry', Marx, J. (ed.), *Propagande et contre-propagande religieuse* (Brussels, 1987).

VERACHTERT, F. & LUYTEN, L. (ed.), *Voorsale des Hemels ofte het begijnhof in de XVII Provinciën* (Retie, 1973).

VERCOUILLIE, J., 'De oorsprong van de naam der Begijnen', *Oostvlaamsche Zanten* 4 (1929) 105-108.

VERDEYEN, P., 'Le procès d'inquisition contre Marguerite Porète et Guiard de Cressonessart (1309-1310)', *Revue d'Histoire Ecclésiastique* 81 (1986) 47-94.

VERMUYTEN, F., *Onze Vlaamse begijnhoven* (Antwerp, 1973).

VERSPRILLE, A.J., 'Het groote- of St. Agnietenbegijnhof', *Leidsch Jaarboekje* (s.l., 1935).

VERVOORT, A., *Beghynken van Mechelen daer den reghel inne staet, hoe elc beghinnende goed mensche sal comen totter volmaectheyt der deuchden* (Antwerp, 1634).

'T VLAAMSCH VOLK (ed.), 'Uit boeken, Brieven en Bladeren: begijnhof van Loon', *'t Daghet in den Oosten* 14 (1898) 129.

WEYERGANS, F. & ZENONI, A., *Béguinages de Belgique* (Brussels, 1972).

WORMGOOR, I., 'De vervolging van de Vrijen van Geest, de begijnen en begarden', *Nederlands archief voor kerkgeschiedenis* 65 (1985) 107-130.

WYNANTS, M. et al., *Begijnen en begijnhoven (Tentoonstelling Algemeen Rijksarchief Brussel, oktober 1994)*, Algemeen Rijksarchief en Rijksarchief in de Provinciën. Educatieve dienst. Dossiers. 2de reeks, 8 (Brussel 1994).

WYTSMANS, C., *Des Béguinages en Belgique* (Gent, 1862).

ZIEGLER, J.E., 'The Curtis Beguinages in the Southern Low Countries and Art Patronage', *Bulletin de l'Institut Historique Belge de Rome* 57 (1987) 31-70.

ID., 'The Curtis Beguinages in the Southern Low Countries: Interpretation and Historiography', *Bulletin de l'Institut Historique Belge de Rome* 59 (1989) 31-70.

ID., *Sculpture of Compassion: The Pieta and the Beguines in the Southern Low Countries (c.1300- c.1600)*, Belgisch Instituut te Rome. Studies over kunstgeschiedenis, 6 (Brussels, 1992).

ID., 'Secular Canonesses as Antecedent of the Beguines in the Low Countries: An Introduction to Some Older Views', *Studies in Medieval and Renaissance History* 13 (1992) 117-135.

ID., 'Some Questions Regarding the Beguines and Devotional Art', *Vox Benedictina* 3 (1986) 338-357.